HANDING ON THE FIRE

Making Spiritual Direction Ignatian

Joseph A. Tetlow, S.J

Library of Congress Control Number: 2021939177
ISBN: 978-1-947617-13-1

Institute of Jesuit Sources
at the Institute for Advanced Jesuit Studies
Boston College
140 Commonwealth Avenue
Chestnuthill Hill, MA 02467, USA

Email: iajs@bc.ed
http://jesuitsources.bc.edu

INSTITUTE FOR ADVANCED JESUIT STUDIES
BOSTON COLLEGE

This book was written
for the New Emmaus Group,
mature disciples of Christ,
lay men and women who prepared
by prayer and study to share their faith
by preaching the Ignatian weekend retreat.

Our Lady of the Oaks Jesuit Retreat House,
Grand Coteau, Louisiana

TABLE OF CONTENTS

About this book

The great composer Gustav Mahler claimed this: "Tradition is not the worship of ashes, but the preservation of fire." This book is about the tradition of *Spiritual Exercises,* which do not just preserve the fire of love of God in Christ, but pass it on.

A layman created the *Spiritual Exercises* for just that purpose, to pass on the fire of love that God had planted in his heart. Ignatius of Loyola guided others through them to help ordinary women and men shake off sinful habits and cultural pressures and grow truly free in "seeking and finding what God wishes in their life."[1] The "life" was, from the beginning, the daily lives of housekeepers, artisans, some religious, and scholars Master Ignatius was living among in Manresa, Barcelona, Alcalá, and Salamanca. He believed that God wanted every person to live holy, growing steadily more in grace, and spreading divine love in their life world.

Very few of those Master Ignatius helped with his *Exercises* went into a monastery or the priesthood. Most remained where they had been before the retreat; but their lives were changed. The spirituality that his contemporaries learned in their retreats was meant to shape the lives they were living—and consequently shape their lifeworld, too. This spirituality is a "lay spirituality" in that its aim and purpose is building the Kingdom of Heaven on earth by putting the fire of love for God and neighbor into each willing heart.

The fire in this lay spirituality has spread remarkably during the fifty-five years since the Second Vatican Council, principally through *Spiritual Exercises* in their several basic forms.[2] Everywhere in North America, movements have brought large numbers of people to experience one-to-one directed retreats in daily life. These retreats left mature disciples wanting to deepen their interior lives in prayer and discernment, and to pass on this experience to others (as happened from the start). Many are applying it to ministries in works of justice, schools, and universities. A surprising number have felt called to offer Ignatian spiritual direction. So new directors have been being trained in solid programs that hand on Ignatian spirituality's principles, norms, and practices.

These Ignatian programs are usually a series of workshops and seminars spread over two or three years and can seem more a training than a formation. I have found over the past forty years that participants complete these programs and begin directing with a sense of competence. I have also found that the new directors are less content with their formation in spirituality and seek to go deeper into its way of proceeding in following Christ. As they direct, the mature have to reflect on their own interior lives and its shape in their tempestuous life world. Consequently, creating programs to help with those purposes has proven a real challenge in our busy and noisy lifeworld.

I have written this book for those mature disciples who are already giving Ignatian spiritual direction. I have in mind also those who offer to form and mentor them and to make their practice of spiritual direction Ignatian. I do not here design a program but just try to lay out the theology in action—the principles, norms, and practices that characterize living Ignatian spirituality—and that has to inform any such program.

This needs doing, for the spirituality that emerges from the experience of *Spiritual Exercises* emerges into a world very different from Ignatius'. He lived and worshipped in real villages; we live and worship in a metaphorical "world village." Consciousness differs, attention is fragmented by media, and possibilities have multiplied exponentially through 500 years of accelerating growth. Yet the spirituality continues faithful to the principles, norms, and practices that shaped it from the beginning and that Master Ignatius tried to capture in the brief notes that are the text of *Spiritual Exercises.*

The spirituality, however, is found not in the text, but in the experience of a life-shaping dialogue with God our Creator that the text's authentic application shapes and enables. Master Ignatius' lay experiences of God gave him knowledge that the director of a retreat stays out of the Holy Spirit's way, "allowing the Creator to deal directly with the one being created and the one being created directly with the Creator."[3] This is the radical idea behind *Spiritual Exercises:* every single believer can "deal directly with the Creator."

The seeker who embraces Ignatian spirituality chooses to keep that dialogue with God our Lord going, lifelong. This is the source of the fire that is passed along, and it has to be stoked by what can be well described as "a disciplined asceticism of love of God and neighbor"—and of self.[4]

Though functioning in a very different world, this human, earthy asceticism is still what it was in Ignatius' day. It still shapes the ongoing dialogue between each seeker and the Creator, and then goes on to shape the many dialogues among each seeker's human relationships. That many mature men and women are living it and guiding others to live it is evidence of the continued vitality and power of the disciplined asceticism of love that we call Ignatian spirituality.

I pray that this book might be a help to all who embrace it.

❖

The book is divided into three parts. The first lays out the practical theology that is the life of the *Spiritual Exercises.* It also explores from several angles the graced experience we call *Ignatian spirituality,* its foundations and principles.

The second part deals directly with the practice of Ignatian spiritual direction. Its first section deals with how any spiritual director listens to a seeker. Its second section deals with the Ignatian way of proceeding in listening to a seeker—with what we specifically listen for. And its third second deals with "the other seeker in the room," that is, with the Ignatian spiritual director's own sense of vocation and interior life.

The third part rather rashly attempts to describe how Ignatian spirituality is actually being experienced and lived out by a great number of mature disciples of Christ whom I have been tasked and privileged to listen to and to share with. I began listening seriously with my ordination to the priesthood in 1960. And since I had begun living Ignatian spirituality in 1947, I have been shaped by and contributed to the radical changes detailed in *The Twentieth Century Construction of Ignatian Spirituality: A Sketch.* [5]

While this construction was in progress, another development foreseen by Karl Rahner, SJ, was in progress. He saw two ways opening up: "The devout Christian of the future will either be a 'mystic'—someone who has 'experienced something'—or will cease to be anything at all."

Ignatian names those devout Christians who have "experienced something." And those who haven't are the nones, the periphery to which our Jesuit first General Apostolic Preference points us. The call to Ignatian spiritual direction is not a trivial pursuit.

A New Beginning

PART ONE

Principles in Ignatian Spirituality

Introduction

The principles in Ignatian spirituality are the great truths in scripture and tradition that Ignatian spirituality emphasizes. About God our Creator and Lord, for instance: we recognize God as the ultimate Truth and the source of beauty and goodness. But we tend to emphasize that God is constantly at work in His creation, inviting us to labor along with Him to build a kingdom of justice, peace, and love, and giving us the gifts to work at it. Again, about ourselves: we recognize that we are created to love God with our whole heart, and to love and care for His magnificent creation. But we tend to emphasize each person's inviolable dignity and every baptized person's summons to contribute lovingly to their life world's justice and peace, starting with their intimate lives and relationships.

All of the Church's great traditional spiritualities, excepting the most extreme, combine a high idealism with a hard-headed practicality. Ignatian spirituality is perhaps outstanding in insisting on what Ignatius knew instinctively. This "practicality" means that the personal holiness of the individual of itself affects their lifeworld. In principle, that's what it means to be practical—it has to make something happen. So we are leery of the current emphasis on the *self* and on *authenticity* and individual *rights*. For we, *who are many, are one body in Christ, and individually we are members one of another,* and we are urged to live as though we believe it.[6]

In principle, Ignatian spirituality has created community—belonging together, being companions—from its very inception in the first Companions of Jesus. For some time in the West, we had grown careless of the power it has to create communion. But since the Council, we have begun thinking of those who follow Ignatian spirituality as *persons for others*. And with the successive popes, we have come to see plainly that Jesus' Sermon on the Mount means that *faith does justice*. The Coronavirus plague hammered home that we are all in this together, whether we are glad to think of it or not.

This is high idealism, and it is entirely practical. It was first expressed by Pedro Arrupe, SJ, as General of the Jesuits. In an address about our ministry in the schools, he defined this general principle:

> Today our prime educational objective must be to form men-and-women-for-others; men and women who will live not for themselves but for God and his Christ—for the God-human who lived and died for all the world; men and women who cannot even conceive of love of God which does not include love for the least of their neighbors; men and women completely convinced that love of God which does not issue in justice for others is a farce.[7]

The "others" might currently raise images of men and women fighting for their rights. But this "being for others" rises first out of our most intimate relations and lives. It then extends to our necessary relationships and to the needy in our lifeworld. And, as Fr. Arrupe said, if our love does not reach acting for peace and justice, it's "a farce."

In our own spiritual lives, therefore, and in the Ignatian spiritual direction we offer, we are keenly aware of how prayer nourishes daily life. For the God we seek is a busy God, creating all things from each atom, to the life of each human, and to the far reaches of space whose outer perimeter we have not yet found.

And this God is also busy shaping each one of us. As Master Ignatius put it: "Few people understand what God would accomplish in them if they were to abandon themselves wholly into God's hands and if they were to allow God's grace to mold them."[8]

This principle about God's intentions and powers has not been changed by the 500 years of discoveries and developments that separate us from the date on the letter.

1. Kenneth Raymond's Story Explains this Book.

Kenneth Raymond was a successful business man, married with two children.[9] When he decided to retire early, he knew he faced further decisions and needed help beyond his weekend retreats. At the Jesuit retreat house, he had heard about the 19th Annotation retreat. So he asked the Jesuit director how to do it and the two of them promptly started.

Kenneth prayed seriously through the Weeks, and to his surprise and profound gratitude, felt himself summoned to a personal relationship with Jesus. He finally grasped how he had been doing God's will all along by finding Him in his family life and work. He also found God calling him and his spouse to some consequential choices.

Most surprising of all to him, he found what he was called to do in his retirement: he was to get others among his friends and parishioners to make this retreat. With the director's encouragement, Kenneth had begun gathering a group even before he had finished his own retreat. He organized their gatherings and talked individually with some of them from time to time. For a while, his Jesuit director met with the group as he mentored Kenneth.

As the group progressed, the director met with them less and less. He was confident that Kenneth was guiding them well, and told him so. Kenneth, for his part, was candid with the director: he found almost as much grace in helping others as he'd found in his own retreat. Yet he somehow wished he had further help in developing his own spiritual life—there were so many experiences others reported that challenged him.

One of the consequential decisions Kenneth was called to make in his own retreat took him and his family to another part of the country. They promptly got involved in a lively parish and began helping others in need. They were not there a year, though, before Kenneth and his spouse were helping other parishioners through the Annotation 19 Exercises.

Men and women all around the nation have stories like this to tell. As they grew more numerous, they and their directors began organizing programs to train guides to give the Annotation 19 retreat. They naturally extended the programs to train spiritual directors.

Those who go through these programs rarely complain. Further, their experiences have steadily drawn both religious and laity to write books helping prayer and direction. There is one general limitation to these programs, though. Their duration and content have the feel rather of handing on a technical skill than of offering a deeper spiritual formation.

What Kenneth wanted was help to go further into his own spirituality, by now quite entirely Ignatian. This help, he did not find a quarter-century ago. It is still hard to find. And that is Kenneth's story.

❖

It is also the story of this book. I learned when working with Kenneth Raymond that preparing materials for Annotation 19 retreats was a good beginning, but only a beginning. I learned that mentoring new guides helped, but we needed something more. We needed programs designed as formation not only of guides as guides, but of guides as mature disciples, themselves. It has taken a while, so not many have lived and ministered through all the steps.

Large numbers of mature lay Catholics first grew serious about the interior life some sixty years ago, with the Council. At the same time, our culture was turning to individualistic concern for the *self,* and psychotherapy became more needed and more common. So we had to learn to distinguish spiritual direction from therapy. Jesuit John English, in his ground-breaking *Spiritual Freedom,* 1973, felt he had to begin with a long chapter distinguishing spiritual direction from psychological therapy.[10] And as we were all learning ways of praying and of living contemplative in the family and the marketplace, mature lay disciples began seeking spiritual direction in greater and greater numbers.

Jesuits William Barry and William Connolly, trained therapists and spiritual directors, laid out in 1982 the essential lines of spiritual direction in their classic *The Practice of Spiritual Direction.*[11] They definitively established the purpose of spiritual direction: giving help to seekers in their relationship with God. The authors honored the stress of their time and stayed close to prayer and the seeker's interior life, setting aside everyday business.

Four decades later, however, the seeker who comes for Ignatian spiritual direction typically has a serious prayer life that both grows out of their daily experience and also helps them interpret their experiences. This is challenging, for the new millennium has brought juddering changes in family, Church, and civil life. Adult children drift away from the Church. Clerical pederasty has stained the Church's holiness. Church teaching confronts flat contradiction in our culture: easy divorce, harsh treatment of immigrants and refugees, the death penalty.

Consequently, seekers want direction as they pray their way through complex decisions and interpret their spiritual experiences in the busyness of ordinary life. In Ignatian spiritual direction, they are called on to address both prayer and daily living. So what I write here tries to handle the *experience of a full life lived according to Ignatian spirituality.* Pastoral counseling will help solve their problems; Ignatian direction will help them discern their own way to find what God means for them to do with every problem.

For this reason, the common matter in Ignatian direction is now spiritual discernment in prayer and daily life. At times, this discernment may be of spirits. But for the most part, in our day, it is Ignatian discernment—coming to decision after prayerful attention to head, heart, and hand. For this spirituality engages the whole person in finding God in all things. As Pope Francis once put it: "It's fundamental that one thinks what one feels and does; feels what one thinks and does; and does what one thinks and feels."[12]

That's a lot to talk about even in a routine spiritual direction conversation.

Touchstones

- Lay women and men are directing *Spiritual Exercises* and giving spiritual direction.

- The purpose of spiritual direction is to help seekers in their relationship with God.

- New directors need and seek help in deepening their own relationship with God.

- The Ignatian director helps the whole person prayerfully discern the next good thing as they try to find God in all things.

- Laity and religious run programs to train Ignatian spiritual directors. These must expand to offer spiritual formation to new directors.

2. What Makes Spirituality Ignatian

Before looking into Ignatian spiritual direction, we'll do well to take a fresh look at Ignatian spirituality, itself.

We know that this spirituality is rooted in the *Spiritual Exercises*. But we will not find it in that text. We find the spirituality in the *dynamic experience* of these Exercises. We experience being in and with God during many hours of intense prayer that thread through the Ignatian retreat.[13] When we continue that thread in everyday life, we are living Ignatian spirituality.

That thread is an ongoing, dynamic dialogue between a human person and Almighty God. In our prayer, we enter into an intimate dialogue, boldly but reverently speaking to our Lord "as one friend speaks to another."[14] Ignatius emphasized this miracle of grace: "it is better when seeking God's will that the Creator and Lord directly communicate Himself to the deeply committed person, embracing them in His love."[15]

Each one who makes the Exercises responds to familiarity with God in their own way.[16] But all are invited to consider God's project of a Kingdom on earth. We begin living this spirituality when we pray the *Suscipe: Take, Lord, and receive all my liberty...*, and choose to bring His kingdom into our own lifeworld.[17]

Of the partners in this dialogue, the One is infinite and all powerful, and we are entirely finite and limited. That almost everything we know about this relationship concerns ourselves must not hide an immensely consoling reality: God the Lord initiates this dialogue. The Lord comes to His people and, in infinite love, to each one He is currently creating.[18]

Then, in a loving move as though to level the ground we stand on in our dialogue with God, He comes to us in Jesus Christ. He lays the foundation for all dialogue He will find acceptable by giving us *the way, the truth, and the life*.[19] As we ponder this in experiencing *Spiritual Exercises*, we come to realize that what we immaturely accepted as Church teaching has now become my personal belief: that *no one can lay a foundation other than the*

One already laid, Jesus Christ.[20] Then we want to live that as completely as we can, like St. Paul: *For me, to live is Christ.*[21]

All Christians are free and enabled by grace to have a dialogue with God. But the dialogue described as the *dynamic experience* of *Spiritual Exercises* is unique. For we entered into it according to the Annotations and Additions—all the principles, norms, and practices detailed in the text. We stand in God's presence, we talk with Christ "as with a friend," we ask for a grace, and expect to find God in everything. Inigo de Loyola had developed these procedures from his own experience of the dialogue and from helping others enter into it. Ignatius prayed that every retreatant would sustain this familiarity with God, aware of the need for discerning spirits and practicing of the Examen.

❖

From our structured experience of God in the *Spiritual Exercises,* then, we have begun to learn how to listen to and respond to God our Lord. We may have felt how God our Lord wants to continue the intimate dialogue after the retreat. It can feel daunting: God wants to continue this intimate conversation with each of us—with *me.* We know that we are free to continue it—to continue it keenly and intensely—to continue it slackly—or not to continue it at all. And if we choose to continue, we are likely to stay with the way we have developed in the Exercises.

And then, as the dynamic dialogue during the retreat was enabled and sustained by the principles, norms, and practices detailed in the text, so will the spirituality in daily life be in appropriate measure. It is important to realize that these three—principles, norms, and practices—are not simple how-to-do-it lists, but the description of a way of proceeding. We are not following a set of printed directions like a list of steps to get onto Zoom.

We are following the wisdom handed on person-to-person from the beginning. During the first twenty-five years of giving and making *Spiritual Exercises*, there were no printed directions. There was no official text. In hundreds of retreats between 1530 and 1548, many new directors handed on the fire in *Spiritual Exercises* by just following their own notes from their own retreats. Master Ignatius finally submitted his own notes for the Church's approval and *Spiritual Exercises* were approved by Pope Paul III in 1548.[22] Even then, the "official text" spread slowly.

This certainly emphasizes the total trust Master Ignatius placed in each retreatant's experience, though it should not make us think less of the text. He judged that what they handed on—what we still hand on—is not an organized collection of someone else's ideas and practices. That would be handing on just another text, "the worship of ashes." What we hand on is a fire—our own living experience of faith-filled prayer, petitions and colloquies, choices made and enacted, all offered to God who is working in and through us. This is how Ignatian spirituality continues to thrive in the world.

Touchstones

- Ignatian spirituality flows not from the text, but from the experience of *Spiritual Exercises.*

- In *Spiritual Exercises,* we experience a dialogue between God and His creature, between infinite freedom and a finite freedom—the "dynamic" of the Exercises.

- The dynamic is enabled and shaped by the principles, norms, and practices of the *Exercises.*

- When the retreat ends, the seeker is free to continue the dialogue with God shaped by the dynamic of *Exercises.*

- And that is the fire handed on in Ignatian spirituality.

3. Why We Make Spiritual Direction Ignatian and How

Before the Second Vatican Council, faithful Catholics' interior lives were strengthened by the sacraments of Reconciliation and Communion and by devotions like the rosary, novenas, and Benediction. All along, though, mature disciples were seeking a deeper spiritual life. Some embraced the life of a religious Third Order, a centuries-old tradition among Franciscans, for instance, and Carmelites and Benedictines. Several generations ago that deeper spirituality became possible for mature disciples in another tradition: the Ignatian.

It began in an organized way in the United States when the first Cenacle opened in 1892. In the Cenacles and the Jesuit retreat houses that quickly followed, Catholic lay men and women listened for three or four days to presentations of the spirituality that runs through *Spiritual Exercises.* The principle was made clear: they were not to sit passively but were invited to develop their own personal relationship with God the Lord. They prayed about it on their own in a long silence—a kind of silence and prayer they could enjoy at no other time in their year. During thirteen decades, thousands returned year after year. They still do, claiming that the annual experience is an anchor for their spiritual lives.

The mainstay of this way of handing on the fire in Ignatian spirituality was the preached weekend retreat. Its series of conferences to the gathered retreatants combined instruction and exhortation. But spiritual formation was deepened by one-to-one conferences. Retreatants cherished having Ignatian spiritual directors and kept them busy during the whole retreat.[23]

The traditional preached weekend retreat continues. Retreatants still seek Ignatian spiritual direction. The climate has changed considerably, though, as "spirituality" has become a commonplace interest in American culture. Other methods of direction have emerged and spread, some from other religious traditions and some based only on human nature. So we have to distinguish Ignatian spiritual direction for the sake of the many serious people who have experienced *Spiritual Exercises* and seek it.

❖

A ground-breaking shift gives us a further reason to clarify how spiritual direction is Ignatian. For about a hundred years starting in the 1880s, Jesuits, Oblates (OMV), and Cenacle Sisters were the only Ignatian spiritual directors.[24] And the *Exercises* were offered only in their retreat houses. A great shift came when the experience of *Spiritual Exercises* moved out of these houses into daily life. A little more than forty years ago, men and women began making *Spiritual Exercises in Daily Life,* directed one-to-one.[25] As a widespread movement, this was a new thing in the American Catholic Church.

As the movement began in the 1980s, the guides were still religious men and women. But very promptly the lay men and women who had made the *Exercises* began handing them on.[26] Then laity were giving Ignatian Exercises and as a matter of course, were giving spiritual direction. When the movement first started, they were prepared for neither. So to meet that need, lay and religious leaders set up programs like St. Louis' BRIDGES and that at The Most Holy Trinity Ignatian Spirituality Center in San José.[27]

Now these programs have spread all over the country and are easily found. They are anchored in parishes, universities, and dioceses; they are freestanding with directors and boards; they are sponsored by a religious order. And they are hardly uniform.[28] One great division is between programs that just offer Retreats in Daily Life and programs that also prepare guides to hand it on. The preparation, however, is usually more like a training than a spiritual formation.

By and large, all programs agree on one point: only those who have made *Exercises* can direct them or give Ignatian spiritual direction. For handing on a spirituality is not like teaching trigonometry. It is not like handing on a technique in cabinetmaking. Giving direction is more like teaching a language: a good Spanish teacher thinks in and speaks Spanish. Or training singers: a good voice coach cannot just tell a student how to ring out *O Sole mio!* but must show how it's done with proper breathing and projection.

That is how it is with a spirituality. A good director, one who passes on Ignatian spirituality authentically and well, already lives it. This spirituality is a particular way of *being* in Christ, a way of proceeding that engages the whole self, head, heart, and hands. This is a way of being united to a *busy* God, the God at each instant creating, redeeming, bringing justice and love. Self leadership first.

Hence, moving into Ignatian directing requires that a mature disciple have reached a disciplined self-awareness, able to attend with open mind and heart to another seeker's spiritual experience. This requires formation and mentoring. And even those who have been guiding for a while know to have our own spiritual director and to be enterprising about our own ongoing formation.

Touchstones

- The movement to Ignatian spiritual direction began in retreat houses.

- The move to Exercises in Daily Life brought lay men and women to direct the retreats and to give Ignatian spiritual direction.

- This movement required giving lay directors formation in Ignatian spirituality.

- Now programs are widely available that form others in the Ignatian tradition of spiritual direction.

4. Handing on What Fire?

The first contemplation in the *Spiritual Exercises* asks us to experience "my immortal spirit like a prisoner in this body that will decay, and my whole self—I mean like an exile in this dark valley among brute beasts."[29] This text seems to come from a pretty dark pessimist who doesn't much love the world. It's as though he sees the world we live in "mainly as 'a proximate occasion to sin.'"[30]

But though Ignatius was a man of his times, after the illumination God gave him at the River Cardoner, he looked on the world as good and full of marvels.[31] When he became head of the Society of Jesus, He used to sit on the roof in the Roman dark and weep at the beauty of the heavens. In the daytime, he revered every human being as God's creation and Christ's triumph—prostitute as well as prince. And he put at the end of *Spiritual Exercises* an exercise that invites a profound experience of God dwelling in and on fire with love for His creation.

In this "Contemplation for Love," Master Ignatius ventures for the first and only time in the text to tell us what he thinks God wants to do: "Everything suggests that this same Lord of mine wishes— as far as He can, according to His divine design—to give me *Himself*."[32] Ignatius lived so aware of God our Lord's incessant creating and provident care that he seems to have attended only occasionally to the scholastic distinction between natural and supernatural.[33] Spiritual directors today may feel in seekers a similar inability to separate natural and supernatural. Somehow, the feel for God working actively in everyday life makes honoring the distinction less urgent than handling the tension between being reasonably in control and humbly waiting on the Lord.

The principle truth is that God really is at all times my Creator and always at work. But the complex world intrudes. That first meditation of Exercises shows that Ignatius lived fully alert to the persistence of evil in this beautiful kingdom, and the mature disciple is sobered by realizing it. Ignatius lived discerning good spirits and bad spirits, and it was a bad spirit that hovered over pagan peoples. All Christians feared the eternal fate of the unbaptized—Hell, forever—and Ignatius acted on that belief. He was on fire to save the pagan peoples and sent missionaries to the world's peripheries to bring Christ. At times, we now lament, some European Christians felt that they needed to destroy pagan cultures to save souls.

But the Church has grown away from that and now views the kingdom of earth differently: What Christ wants of our cultures is their ultimate triumph—our world transmuted from sin to grace, fully realizing the splendors God intends for it. This is liberation theology: "The Christian involves himself in the building up of the human city, one that is to be peaceful, just, and fraternal, and acceptable as an offering to God."[34]

That helps as a vision for the future, but we are still confounded by the persistence of "the problem of evil" in the present. We still have to discern how we can pass on the fire of divine love in the whirlwind of our sinful human life. A declaration by the Second Vatican Council will help.

> This is a fact that only those who believe can grasp: The earthly city and the heavenly city interpenetrate each other. It remains a mystery of human history—a history which sin will keep in great disarray until the full splendor of God's children is finally revealed.[35]

The bishops did not mean that there are two kingdoms, one good and the other bad. No: each of two kingdoms is God's creation and the Creator is at work in each of them—the kingdom of earth and the kingdom of heaven. We live our lives wholeheartedly in Christ's kingdom, yet each of us remains for this time a member of the kingdom of earth. Christ's disciples pay taxes and obey laws as an evangelical duty: *For there is no authority except from God.*[36] Each of us walks with one foot in the kingdom of earth and one in the kingdom of heaven.

This would be clear enough except for this "mystery of human history"—sin. For "sin will keep in great disarray" the unfolding stories of these two intertwined kingdoms—sin is in the stories of *both* kingdoms— "until the full splendor of God's children is finally revealed." That moment will seal the history of both kingdoms.

More intimately, meanwhile, the mystery of sin plays out in each of us. For we take to ourselves the good things of the earthly kingdom—and sin along with them. A good image is having a fine steak, enjoying what is laced with synthetic growth hormones, nitrates, and persistent antibiotics. Or drinking river water that's purified but still laced with deadly lead. Thus, sin-in-the-world around me becomes sin-in-me. And then I approve of it and it's my sin, as I ingest the poison and it becomes my poison.

These intertwined kingdoms form the frame for our prayer to discern the next good thing to do. We must live discerning how we might pass on the fire, the great Good News of God's merciful love. St. Paul explained to the Romans how the mature do this: *Do not conform your behavior to the present age, but be transformed by the renewing of your minds, so that you may discern for yourselves what is good and acceptable and perfect.*[37] But Paul did not make this up: Jesus had challenged *the whole multitude: Why do you not judge for yourselves what is right?*[38]

We live a spirituality unremittingly engaged with the kingdom of earth, a spirituality for the marketplace. But this spirituality guides us to strengthen the kingdom of heaven in our marketplace not first by social or political action, but by living a disciplined asceticism of love of God and neighbor and self.

And if we will, we can appreciate this love as a fire in our hearts that we want to pass on.

Touchstones

- Ignatius' mystical illumination left him convinced of the goodness and beauty of all of creation, in which God continues at work.

- The experience of the *Contemplation* helps us accept the great human dignity bestowed on humankind by God's wanting to give Himself to us.

- The Council declared: The kingdom of heaven and the kingdom of earth, spoiled by sin, interpenetrate.

- The seeker who lives Ignatian spirituality constantly discerns progress in spreading a kingdom of justice, peace, and love. This is a fire in our hearts.

5. The Purpose of Ignatian Spiritual Direction

"A spiritual director," an old definition explains, "is someone to whom others go for spiritual direction." And a good spiritual director? "Someone to whom others keep on going."

Well and good. But what do they do when they get there? What are the purposes of going to a spiritual director?

A seeker ordinarily comes to talk about their purposes in life and about their prayer. The seeker's direct focus may be on praying better or "finding myself." A good director's focus is always on the seeker's relationship with God.

Early on in this country, both seekers and directors focused strongly on prayer. "Not that directors have little or no interest in the rest of a person's life," Barry and Connolly noted, but "the focus of interest is the directee's experience of God or of something that points to God."[39]

This focus required close personal attention, feasible only in one-to-one conferences. When laity began seeking it, the clergy best prepared to do extensive work one-to-one and to teach others to do it were trained therapists, who gave us a well developed model of working one-to-one.

We used the language of therapy and learned from its procedures. We called seekers our "directees." We established the therapist's "working alliance" between us. We watched for "resistance" during a spiritual conversation and "transference" between director and seeker.[40] Spiritual experience seemed to be what went on in a person's psychological life.

This was unavoidable fifty years ago not only because of the therapeutic model, but also because of our culture's individualism. Everyone interpreted life in terms of the individual's experience.[41] Sociologists studied the isolated member of *The Lonely Crowd*.[42] American Catholics were also members of the *MeGeneration,* steeped in what Christopher Lasch called *The Culture of Narcissism*. We were all—directors as well as seekers—deeply individualistic.

In these beginnings, we didn't yet know what it took for a person "in the world" to develop a lively interior life and prayer. A number of Third Order members did it but their witness was quiet, as though they were living a monastic life at home. Further—on the model of therapy—we were all then thinking that "spiritual growth is basically interior," as Barry and Connolly taught us.[43] We knew, of course, that spiritual growth had to show itself in action; but we considered "these external indices ... in their appropriately secondary place."[44]

❖

That could not last in the Ignatian tradition. Since the God we seek is a busy God, we cannot let our interior life and prayer float above our daily life in our lifeworld. Our spiritual life does not free us from our flesh—how could it if we receive Christ in Communion? Rather, our spiritual life roots in the experience of God freeing us from our sin so that we can *present our bodies*—and everything we experience in a day, lifelong—*as a living sacrifice, holy and acceptable to God, which is our spiritual worship.*[45]

We've known that all along, of course. But in this new millennium, we have grown more aware of how God embeds us in humanity as well as in the Mystical Body, which can feel vaguely immaterial. It is not immaterial: The Mystical Body is *us*. It's us in a flourishing nation full of thriving, creative, hungry, and impoverished people. We cannot let our spirituality or our political ideas and social prejudices trump Jesus' message: *I was hungry and you fed me.*[46] Pope Francis considers feeling individually saved apart from the people a new kind of Gnosticism—the heresy that separates mind from body.[47] Popes have written not only about faith and hope in God, but also about making peace, caring for refugees, defending the earth—and even about *The Theology of the Body.*[48] They are expressing the *sensus fidelium,* what Christ's disciples really believe. It shows in the fact that the seekers who come for spiritual direction act as whole persons. So do those who give it.

Now we can consider the purpose of Ignatian spiritual direction. It is about prayer but not just about prayer. It is also about all of our experience when we cross the threshold between prayer and everyday life. Then our compounded experiences are the *good fruit that comes from making the tree sound.*[49] These good fruits are rooted in prayer and self-examination, but they are actually loving works and good habits—the enactment of the gifts shared in us by God.

The *good fruit* is the work of head and heart and hand, all three, not of only one or the other. We therefore have to discern the good we are to do. So the purpose of Ignatian spiritual direction is to strengthen and guide how a seeker interprets the dynamic interplay of head, heart, and hand. For as the pope has pointed out, what we do is what we think and feel; what we feel is what we think and do; and what we think is what we do and feel.

Ignatian spiritual direction serves the whole human person. And it is given by a whole human person, too.

Touchstones

- All spiritual direction focuses directly on the seeker's relationship with God our Lord.

- Ignatian spiritual direction focuses on the seeker's ongoing dialogue with God as the seeker co-creates with the Creator the two kingdoms.

- Our ongoing dialogue with God our Creator and Lord goes on in our prayer and in all that we think about and do—the totality of our experience.

- Ignatian spiritual direction, therefore, attends to both: our prayer and to our enactment of its fruits in everyday life.

- Strengthening and guiding a seeker's ongoing discernment marks Ignatian spiritual direction.

6. My Self in Ignatian Spirituality

"At the heart of an understanding of Christian spirituality," Richard Hauser wrote in *Life in the Spirit,* "is an adequate understanding of the self."[50] In the Elder Mullan translation, Master Ignatius uses the word 166 times: conquer himself, finds himself, exercise himself, humble myself, change himself, perfect himself. Any English translation would be comparable. While Master Ignatius meant something closer to the whole person, or to the soul, we mean something quite different. We'd better attend to that.

Hauser was writing as the 1980s began, when Americans were getting obsessed with the *self.* Not the *soul,* which is our permanent life-principle, but the *self*—who we are *becoming.* Our self is incomplete and each individual has to fulfill, finish, "be myself."[51]

This much, mature disciples can agree with. But Americans grew to believe that each of us has to do this individually, trusting only our own experience to find out what we want to believe and what is right for us to do. So we became isolated and loneliness became a plague among us.[52] By the new millennium, Jesuit John Staudenmaier explained, Americans tended to feel that our real life's project is to create an "authentic" self—this is the real purpose of our living and will bring fulfillment.[53] But it has proven a poor way to live and scholars see it as the source of Americans' anxiety because "who we really are is constantly in question."[54]

The Americans who have made *Spiritual Exercises* ought to have tamed that question. We chose to belong among God's people, to belong to Christ. Like Him, we will *grow in wisdom, age, and grace* as the Spirit guides us. So we readily acknowledge that as selves, we are still in process, not yet finished—but we are more than an unfinished self. We see that in the *Exercises,* which Jesuit Thomas Clarke sees as "an instrument through which individuals would be helped to lose and to find their unique selves."[55] We lose the *self* that belongs only to this life and discover the *self* of the *person* coming to be as a member of Christ's Mystical Body.

Then the spirituality that flows from those revelatory *Exercises* helps us keep mindful of how our faith has shaped the *self* we are coming to be.

First, my *self* is coming to be in God's creation. The Contemplation for Love brought me "aware of how the fullness of our eternal Good dwells in all created things, giving them being, and keeping them in existence with His infinite being and presence." In that Presence, I "enjoy continuous instruction, attention and consolation" in my authentic self.[56] For this ongoing dialogue between us and our Creator is not just in our minds and prayers. It goes on in our whole selves, *temples of an active God*—in us, *the Spirit dwells.* [57] I am in no instant absolutely alone. For my God guides me to enact the gifts poured into me and shapes the events of my life world that shape me. My *self* is incomplete because God isn't finished with me yet.

Second, even incomplete, I am unique and unrepeatable. But I am not isolated: I *belong,* I am a *member* in communion. "All of us begin life within concentric, unchosen relationships," Luma Simms writes, "we are born into a family, a kinship, a city, a nation, a heritage not of our choosing."[58] The choosing is God's; Christ's disciples cannot honestly cherish Him merely in private. "Rather," as Bernard Haring explained, "in the light of faith, they discover the presence of Christ in the world and in the age they live in, just as they have discovered his presence *in their innermost being.*"[59] I am a *self among selves* and a *self for other selves,* because we are companions on a pilgrimage. This grounds our disciplined asceticism of love.

Here is a third reality about my *self* in Ignatian spirituality. We are on a pilgrimage and we have a destiny. Each one of us is surely still coming to be. But we live this life to some purpose beyond isolated self-fulfillment. The Spirit gives each of us a "vocation," a call, a unique work to do. It is not just about my inner life and it is not an arbitrary imposition from outside. God embedded our purpose in our gifts—all the gifts of place and time, of mind and heart, of relatives and loves—that make us the *self* whom God loves. When we enact our gifts, we are becoming the person God longs to live with in eternity and we are building both kingdoms.

This is who I am, one to whom Jesus said, *I have chosen you out of the world,* not to take me out of the world, but for this: *I commission you to go out and to bear fruit, fruit that will last.*[60]

Who we are, then, is not "constantly in question." We are now immortal beings, Christ's people, and our common project and hope is to live so as to bring His kingdom to our lifeworld.

And to be ready to guide others to make progress in belonging to Him, if that is His gift.

Touchstones

- My soul is my life principle and immortal; my self is all of me journeying through time.
- The currently popular sense of self is that I must decide on my own what to believe and do and so become "authentic."
- Ignatian spirituality grounds our sense of self in a personal relationship with God our Creator and Redeemer. We are never alone entirely.
- God gives each of us a mission in life, shaped by the gifts God has given us.

- Some of us are called to be spiritual directors.

- We are persons webbed in relationships and we belong to the community of the Church.

- Christ has chosen us out of the world and commissioned us to complete His work of establishing on earth the kingdom of heaven. This is how we think of ourselves.

7. A Simple Grammar of Experience

The Ignatian spiritual director focuses on seekers' relationships with God. What seekers tell about, however, is their *experiences* in this relationship. So how do we listen to *experiences?*

Actually, mature listeners instinctively follow a way of proceeding when listening to others' experiences, just the way mature talkers instinctively follow grammar rules when talking. In principle, we know that grammar organizes the words we use and the ways they relate. We don't think about them, though; we just talk.

In the same way, we just listen for certain elements we know are at work in any experience. Every *decision* is shaped in its *context,* for instance. And the whole person, in their current *condition,* experiences—a tired working spouse *values* time at home, an alert policeman keeps a *perspective* on a crowd, a dedicated surfer *desires* to find the perfect wave. When we act, then, we are not like a machine doing what it was designed to do, but we are *enacting* these internal and external elements. The whole person experiences, just as the whole person talks.

These are the elements, then, that compose every experience: context, condition, perspective, perception, value, desire, decision, and enactment. When we attend to any one of them, we are looking into the experience through one of its facets, like looking into a large cut diamond. Through the facet into the whole diamond.

We might do this instinctively, but when we are directing, we do well to be more deliberate about it. When we do keep mindful of this "grammar of experience," we do not just hear a story. We are listening for keys to a reasonable interpretation of the experience and getting ready to help find its meaning—and to discern where the seeker's progress might lie.

Consider Carlos's experience of deciding on a new job.[61]

Carlos was born and raised in Houston and is raising his family there. With a good business degree, he has had a good job and been promoted twice to manage more and more people. We had been meeting intermittently for some time and I knew that Carlos prayed regularly and that the Spirit had given him a desire for work that would help people who needed help.

Then, some months ago, Carlos was told that his firm had been bought out. He told me when we met that he was to be downsized with a generous separation package. Months then passed without contact, though I knew that Carlos was very actively searching for the kind of job he thought he wanted. He looked into Church work and to working at a charitable foundation.

Then one day, he called and asked to visit. He was excited and happy—he had just signed a contract for the "perfect job." Here is the experience he came and told about.

The context. Carlos had searched around Houston but he had not found a job that both fitted his management skills and met his hope to spend his time really helping people who needed help. He had used the web in his search, of course.

His condition. Carlos admitted that he had been a bit frightened at first. But he kept faithful to his daily prayer. When he got too anxious, he would remember what one retreat director once said: "Everyone you help in any way, you help Christ—everyone!"

His perspective. This had become his perspective on work: he was to help others in Christ's Name. At first, he had thought this meant working for the Church. But as the weeks went by, his perspective widened. He would try to find work directly helping the poor or people in difficult circumstances. Nothing more specific than that. As he described this experience, I thought that change remarkable but remained silent.

His perception. Carlos was clear-eyed: He needed a job. He saw that he should have an income adequate to raising his children well. Some of the positions he heard about would not give him that.

His values. Carlos was aware of balancing a number of things dear to him. He loved his wife and children and they came first. But because of the way he now valued his work, he put high value on finding a position that would give him good pay and good work for others.

His desires. Those two values focused his desire. He wanted work that would call on his business skill for handling people who really needed help—and that would pay enough to support his family.

His decision. His decision came as a great surprise. He was suddenly offered (recruited for, actually) a position in Little Rock managing the intake office in a small hospital. It seemed a purely secular job. But as he listened to details, he experienced a strong sense of its rightness. He suddenly knew that his training and experience had prepared him to help people this way, not by working in a rectory or a 501(c)3. He would be helping a lot of people who really needed help.

Enactment. Carlos was almost giggling as he told about saying *yes* to himself even before he knew the salary—which turned out to be very adequate. And his spouse was quite content about the move. Finishing those details, Carlos waited for his director's reaction.

As I have mentioned, I was struck by the *perception*—that "great sense of its rightness"—that Carlos had experienced even as this "purely secular" position was being described. So I pointed out to Carlos the many marks of consolation that came after the decision: First, his earlier prayerful change of perspective on whom he should serve prepared him to find what he was looking for in a "purely secular" job. Then, Carlos's own contentment after he had said *yes.* Another consolation was his spouse's agreement and their strong trust that they would find the right schools and good friends in the Lord in Little Rock, a place they had never thought to live in.

These things happened a while back and the few times Carlos has come to visit me, he says that this decision has continued blessings. I couldn't have analyzed all the elements in this experience in the orderly fashion described here. But I had discerned that the consoling *perception*—"the great sense of rightness"—held the key to its meaning. This is how the Grammar of Experience helps in spiritual direction.

Touchstones

- The Ignatian spiritual director is listening to the experience of the seeker's relationship with God in Christ.

- We are still learning how to interpret experiences and need a way of proceeding to be sure we listen well.

- As a mature speaker talks grammatically, a mature listener hears in a sort of grammar of experience.

- The elements of an experience are context, condition, perspective, perception, value, desire, decision, which are known in their enactment.

- We listen for an element that might be the key to the story's meaning and to where the seeker's progress lies.

8. A Disciplined Asceticism of Love of God, Others, and Self

Jesuit theologian James Hanvey points out that a whole-hearted desire to serve Christ and to labor with Him in creating the kingdom requires "a disciplined asceticism of love for God and for neighbor."[62] This asceticism is obviously not living in the desert on locusts and honey. It is living in our chaotic world, managing a well-ordered, purposeful life, mind and heart fixed on loving and serving God first. Every one of us needs to keep at this, for our own salvation and for the good of those we offer direction to.

For this is first of all an asceticism of the *love* we are created for. Ignatius reminds us that love is what is *done*, not just felt or expressed—but *done*.[63] And the thing done is a mutual giving of gifts, including the *self*, back and forth—that means both giving and receiving. Not once for all: because we are limited and sinful, the fullness of love means a lifelong generous effort, an asceticism.

The love in our disciplined asceticism begins in God. God loves to us first, sharing with us being and life, understanding and freedom, and all the things we can know and enjoy. Our ascetical response is accepting His gifts as they come to us. I humbly accept the person my Creator is making me—my time and place, my race and sex and talents. I humbly admit that I am acceptable to God, because He makes me so.

I live my relationship of love for God by obeying His commandments. But in this asceticism, I do not obey in order to get to heaven—though that's a lively matter—but because I love the Lord who commands and I want to please Him by doing what He wants. What He wants, actually, is our fulfillment: *Rejoice always, pray constantly, give thanks in all circumstances; this is the will of God in Christ Jesus for you.*[64] Because it is our fulfillment, it may sound easy. But it is no easy asceticism when lived fully.

For it can be tested, sometimes severely. I feel hate for a political enemy. I cannot forgive a faithless spouse. Here, my discipline is clear: I never deny that I was hurt, I forgive whoever hurt me, and I pray for them. I ask God to forgive me my sins as I have forgiven those who sinned hurting me. This is the confounding discipline Jesus passed on to us.

My human love is *rooted and grounded in love*—the love that Jesus showed for us. I keep begging the grace "to know Him more clearly, love Him more dearly, and follow Him more nearly." And among my leading ascetical practices is prayer on His life, His Passion and death, and His Resurrection. And I humbly believe that He comes to me out of the matter of the earth—Bread and Wine—in Communion. This Communion places me with Him doing God's work on this earth, now.[65]

What God wants done on this earth in my lifetime, Jesus made plain: *You are to love one another the way I loved you.* So Ignatian disciplined asceticism means finding God active in the others whom God has in my life. First are my *necessary relationships*: parents and siblings, aunts and uncles, children and close friends. These, I did not choose but I accept them not just in feeling or claim, but in what I do and say and avoid. That discipline prepares me to love others whom I choose to have in my life.

Jesus showed how. Any time anyone asked for help, He promptly gave it, not considering the cost to Himself. He never cut anyone out of His love—not Nicodemus and not even Judas. From Him, we learn how we sin against love. For instance, we cut off a necessary relation, like the weekly Communicant who cut off a spiteful sibling and had not talked with him in years. Or we just hold someone we should love at arm's length, showing no more love than "How you been?" expresses. Instead of sinning against love, we put good order into visiting elderly parents, caring for an autistic child, or sticking by those who persist in doing what we consider sinful. The mother of a priest who left and married without clearance sat at the wedding in the front row: "He is my son," was her whole explanation.

Finally, while we cannot imagine ourselves free of our culture's self-absorption, we can freely put good order into our lives and grow to be *good trees putting forth good fruit.* For this asceticism uproots selfishness and narcissism, even being self-absorbed in our projects or health. Rather, we properly love ourselves as we love our neighbors, and we treat ourselves as we treat those whom we truly and holily love.

Practically, this means we consciously develop those powers, authorities, and virtues the Spirit infuses in our spirits and we express them in a mature Christian character. We watch what we become attached to: person, work, idea, process. This is where we understand that *for freedom Christ has set us free.*[66] So we work to keep from following half-baked ideas, and resolutely stay free of attachment to an ideology—human theories that pretend to explain everything in a handful of judgments. We learn from our Master: *Learn of me, for I am meek and humble of heart.*[67]

We live discerning lives, giving back to God the best use of our gifts that we can manage. When directing, we try not to react instantly to anything, but rather wait until we can respond. This takes reflection, which can be very brief if we are keeping some good order in our thoughts and desires.

We will manage this only if we pray regularly and—most importantly—if we keep reflecting on our days, what we have thought and felt, said and done.

Another Beginning

PART TWO

Norms in Ignatian Spiritual Direction

Introduction

A "norm" states what we usually do and how we think and feel about it. So in Ignatian spirituality, for instance, it's a norm that we make the Examen—and as a norm, we do it daily. An important norm about discernment is that we pay attention to what we are thinking, what we are feeling, and what we are doing, all three. And perhaps the first of all norms is that we pray to find God in all things and to grow in Christian virtues. These mark our "normal" days.

In roughly the same way, "norms" are the usual patterns in our way of giving spiritual direction. They describe our way of proceeding—how our minds and spirits work as we listen—and what we listen for. In general, these norms indicate how experienced directors proceed—what might be called the "best practices." They point to what matured Ignatian directors do and how we do it.

Some norms are unchanging. Ignatian spiritual direction is best done one-to-one, for instance, and that has been the norm from the beginning. Again, we listen for a good while before we venture to give a seeker a suggestion or advice. And we are careful not to be apodictic, though there are limits: a Commandment is a Commandment, and we will not let a seeker be deceived about obeying it.

Note that this latter norm is sliding over into a principle—one like, "We can know God's will for us"—which cannot be ignored or rationalized. If we honor a principle all the time, then we are "normally" honoring it, and we have a "principle/norm." We could theorize on this for long paragraphs but instead, it's useful to just note the overlap. Together the two give adequate support to sound practice in Ignatian spiritual direction.

Some norms shift and change: principles do not, but norms do. A generation ago, to look at a surprising norm that has changed radically, even the experts did not *direct* individual retreatants, but *preached* even the thirty-day retreat to groups. And not long ago, it was normal to refer to seekers as "clients," which I have not heard recently. So norms in spiritual direction are best thought of as *currently* widespread guidelines on how to listen and question, respond to doubts or developments in grace, and whom to continue seeing.

In the end, the norms add up to our way of proceeding. A simple list of norms would be both unenlightening and boring. Stories will illustrate what can then be put in a Touchstone.

And while we share a great deal, each of us correctly expects to be guided by the Holy Spirit in our way of proceeding. That, praise God, is an unchanging principle/norm.

I. THE FIRST LISTEN: AS THE SEEKER SPEAKS

9. The Current Seeker and What They Want

In all the stories illustrating norms, I will be naming those who come for spiritual direction, "seekers." Who is a seeker and what can we say about them today?

They are what they seem always to have been: mature disciples with a holy longing to know God. From Christianity's beginning, it has moved men and women to consecrated lives and then to organized monasteries. But the holy longing also moved Christians "in the world," and laity applied the monasteries' spiritualities to parenting and working and all the rhythms of daily life in the world.[68]

Seekers who look for Ignatian direction, however, are not looking for a kind of in-the-world monastic spirituality. For as Bernard Haring has observed, mature disciples are caught in a materialist culture not much interested in God, and yet are experiencing God "as a transcendent mystery present in the world and in life itself."[69] They are looking for a spirituality that will help them embrace the Church's turn from its inward concerns to our mission to transform the world.[70]

Seekers today come with a strong yearning to grasp this "transcendent mystery present in the world." So when they tell us they are "looking to do God's will," they are not ordinarily looking for a comfortable way of praying that will leave them in peace. Occasionally, a seeker comes who has not yet even found their path in life. But most seekers who come to us now already live a committed life, single or married. They come for some purpose touching on both prayer and action: one to find deeper prayer in their busyness; another, seeking how to live faithful in a difficult trial; another, downsized and facing the next stage in life.

The seekers who understand Ignatian spiritual direction are seeking God "the transcendent mystery present in the world." They come for direction to get on with it, to feel some growth in their spirits. That growth, an important norm reminds us, will come as God intends. God is moving each seeker who approaches us and our task is to listen so as to help the seeker discern how.

A banker or the working mother of grown children may feel a deep desire to live with a clear conscience and assured peace of heart. A technician may seek greater steadiness in her prayer and increasing depth in her sense of union. A man downsized may have an instinct that God is calling him to serve needy people more directly that he has until now. God calls each single person to make progress in mindset and heartset in the life they now enjoy.

The threads of progress are common: normally, each of these seekers need reconciliation, freedom from attachments and disordered feelings and affections, less needless self-preoccupation, and greater and greater magnanimity in loving those whom God have given them to love.[71] The simplest seeker can actually enact the "third degree of humility," and find joy in their suffering as Jesus did or the Lady Mary.[72]

Catherine, for instance, gave her parish community an example. The mother of growing children, she was offered pity because "she was sick," and responded that she wasn't "sick," she just had cancer. And she discerned that she was with Jesus in suffering the savage chemotherapy. Yet: *Always joyful!*

This discernment was crucial for her. Of course: a seeker comes as an entire person, not just a psyche or a mind, so every seeker needs discernment. We all need to distinguish daily between an inspiration of the good Spirit and an invitation to selfish fulfillment. We can't do this unless we live aware of the dynamic interplay of head, heart, and hand. For God is incessantly active in each of us and might invite us to join Him by an idea, a feeling, a conviction, a deed that, if we choose, will enact "God's will"—and give us the *freedom for which Christ has set us free.*[73]

Touchstones

- The "seeker," today as in all of the Church's history, feels the "holy longing" to know and serve God better.

- Many seekers are looking for clarity in God's will and peace of heart.

- A director listens aware that any seeker may be living in union with Jesus Christ.

- A seeker wants and needs to make progress; the Ignatian director expects to witness it.

- Ultimately every seeker lives toward that freedom brought us by Jesus Christ.

10. Listening Quietly the First Time We Meet a Seeker

A wise spiritual director listens to a seeker every time as though it were the first time. But the actual first time poses challenges.

The seeker may just want help with a problem and we deal with that. But even then, we listen this first time aware of two things. We will have to decide whether Ignatian spirituality can help this person now, and how; and then, we will have to decide whether to accept or suggest continuing to meet.

So to begin with, the spiritual director simply listens to what the seeker is actually saying about themselves, their prayer, and their everyday life. As a norm, we listen in silence. An experienced director might say very little during any conversation. This is useful to the seeker: being listened to attentively frees us to speak our minds and lets us uncover things we might otherwise not have reached.

Our silence helps us directors, too. In a first conversation, being silent gives us space to learn whether this seeker has accepted this truth: *Do you not know that you are God's temple and that God's Spirit dwells in you?*[74] This is a basic spiritual experience. The seeker who has experienced it will display a certain serenity of spirit and in the ordinary course of things will need less guidance. The seeker who has not will usually need more guidance. Noting this helps a director decide whether to continue meeting.

Seekers commonly begin a conversation talking about their prayer. This seems especially the case in their very first visit. We notice first how they practice prayer. We might have to ask: Daily? For how long? How? On what topics or subjects? And do they talk with God "as one friend were speaking with another, or a servant to his master"?[75]

At times, a seeker will wonder "whether I am praying right." They are "praying right" when they are praying the way they *can* pray—considering gifts of mind, spirit, and of situation—and not some way they heard tell about. Our concern here is that they know God in their hearts and that however they pray helps them grow not just in knowing of scripture, but in familiarity with God.

Then, they are "praying right" if the way they are praying keeps them praying. This is the first of two basic norms: the way I am now praying keeps inviting me into prayer. The other basic norm, touched on below, deals with how their prayer weaves into their lives.

The prayer of one kind of seeker I sometimes see (especially during weekend retreats) is not solitary mental prayer, but the prayer of a devout Christian. These seekers might receive Communion daily, go for Reconciliation, recite the rosary or the Chaplet of Mercy, attend hours of Adoration, and have devotions to their saints. A couple of generations ago, Catholics led that kind of intense devotional life.[76] That peaked, Catholic historians point out, roughly in the 1950s.

It was easy sixty years ago to think this "praying right" was somehow second-rate and should be outgrown. I have learned, I think, that the Lord calls some people to this way and I think I am wrong to chivvy them to change. They belong to those Master Ignatius pointed to in Annotation 18, "who want help to be instructed and to come to a certain degree of contentment of soul."[77] I wonder that we could consider ourselves in a position to correct the Spirit who is guiding them.

When they come, Ignatian directors do well to be personally familiar with the program Master Ignatius laid out for them: more instruction than usual with us, the Examen, and a solid set of practices in the text's "Three Methods of Prayer."[78]

❖

It makes sense to start spiritual direction talking about prayer because prayer epitomizes our ongoing dialogue with God. Without attention to prayer, "spiritual direction" is probably pastoral counseling—good help, probably mainly problem-solving, and guided by a different set of norms.

In this first conversation, we may get a sense of where seekers are in their journey, and a little about how their Christian character has unfolded. We need to be alert to differences in the backgrounds and contexts of our two lives. The spiritual experiences of the retired Oklahoma rancher, John, differed from those of his urban director, Laura. He still wore jeans and boots. She was mothering teenagers and holding a job in a bank. Both of them, led by Laura, had to keep aware of the different contexts of their experiences.

One thing we are likely to find out in this first conversation is whether they can recount well their experiences with God. As Barry and Connolly put it: "The only prerequisite for engaging in the type of direction we describe is that the person being directed have affective experiences of God which he notices and which he can talk about with a director."[79]

The "affective experiences of God" referred, fifty years ago, directly to prayer. That has changed pretty thoroughly. Now that Christians are perceiving God intimately creating and redeeming, the "affective experience of God" a seeker recounts might be a beautiful insight in their prayer, but might just as well be a blessed impulse to call a lonely friend. All the years I knew him, for instance, Trey lived hard times, constantly said, "God is always with me," and refused to be discouraged. We have to listen carefully, for we are all still learning how mature disciples leading a busy life can carry on a familiar—even intimate—dialogue with our Creator and Lord.

While there are many other considerations involved, we can hope as this first hour comes to its end to be ready to discern whether to continue spiritual direction with this seeker. The decision can be very consequential.

Touchstones

- In a first conversation with a seeker, we find out whether Ignatian spirituality will help them and whether we can and want to.

- Normally in this first conversation (as in others, later), we stay silent and listen.

- Seekers often begin a conversation by telling about their prayer.

- The seeker is "praying right" if their way keeps them praying and reaches into their daily life.

- We sometimes encounter and direct the seeker Master Ignatius describes in Annotation 18.

- Even in our first conversation, we need to learn something about the seeker's context and their lives.

- Today, seekers tend to be concerned not mainly or directly with help in prayer but with their affective experience of God in everyday life.

11. Listening the First Time to a New Companion in Grace

Shirley waited in the small office to begin what we hoped would be regular spiritual direction. When I joined her and we greeted each other, she thanked me for seeing her and said she was surprised when I had. I said I was happy they could meet and then asked, "Tell me a bit about yourself." She began a rather long story.

As we listen in our first meeting to their stories, we catch the facts in this seeker's life. When we expect to keep meeting, we need to know whether the person is living a married life, works, prays, and is rearing children or has reared them. We want to hear about their religious practices, too. It seems odd to me, but some important things can go unmentioned until after we've needed them to fully understand a seeker's experiences.

Shirley has just celebrated thirty-five years of married life and has three grown children. Two of them are married and have children but only one of them still goes to Mass. She's not sure what the third, a daughter, believes any more.

I could hear the pain in her voice, but chose to remain silent and let Shirley decide what she wanted to explore. She said that they had just moved to another home. They had meant to down-size, but hardly managed because they wanted to have room for the children and grand-children to visit. And they have kept going to their old parish, St. Edward's.

This makes Shirley pause for a moment and then ask, "We were wondering whether that's considered all right?" I had to think for a moment and then pointed out, "The bishop has no problem with it." Shirley began describing one of the pastors. To keep the conversation focused on Shirley, I broke in.

"Before we go on, let me ask what you have in mind about our meeting. Would you like to continue for a while in spiritual direction?" Shirley promptly said that she did—there are a lot of things to talk about. "Is that all right?"

I had now heard what we listen for in a first encounter: the broad outlines of this seeker's life and situation, what they need to talk about, and whether they want to keep going and we think we can and want to help.

Besides these practical questions, we listen carefully for whether this seeker has made the first great discernment that God lives with them and cares for them. Even when they have, many beginners have only a sort of official relationship with God as a good Christian. In this first conversation, we want to find out whether this seeker is "familiar with God"—in the mundane sense of being familiar with another person.

Shirley had made it clear that she was familiar with God and would be able to share her thoughts and feelings. I had caught some intimations about her interior life. It's worth noting that those who cannot do that rarely come for spiritual direction. And occasionally we agree to meet a person who tries but seems not ready to manage it. This is one of the occasions when we have gently to make the first session the only session.

It was not with Shirley. She explained that she had started using the *lectio divina* and had some questions about it. She liked to pray in the morning and that was easy now that the children were all gone and her husband was leaving early for work. For a while, she had used *Sacred Space* on her iPhone but then she changed to the booklet *GIVE US US THIS DAY,* and she just prays with the readings of the day. She likes to say the Morning and the Evening prayers and sometimes her husband joins her in the evening.

With this, I now know that this seeker is familiar with the Lord, prays regularly and how—using the *lectio divina* and needing help with it. I know a bit about the externals of her life and a bit about her contentments and some discontents. This has taken most of an hour.

So I remark that we need to watch the clock and tell Shirley that I will be glad to meet with her for a while to see "how it goes." So we set a day and time in the next month, "right here again—if that's all right?" When she says it's fine, I tell her, "Well, Shirley, it seems to me you're moving along well. I'd keep doing what you're doing. You might want to add a bit of a reflection in the evening on how the Lord has been with you this day to thank Him. But I think the Lord is with you."

❖

The first conversation with a seeker may start not with a long story like Shirley's, but with the hard reality of a problem. For instance, Trey simply dropped in on the director one day when he passed by the retreat house. Trey had listened to the director give the talks of his most recent retreat. He came "just to ask for prayers"—he had lost his job when the work the company did disappeared. He badly needed regular income because he has three daughters to raise—single parent. He shared a bit about picking up odd jobs, but it wasn't really enough.

The director asked about the daughters, hoping to get Trey to talk about himself instead of his problems. He has three, one about to finish college, the others in high school. He declared that he loves them very much and takes care of them—that's his whole life.

But Trey was not ready to open his heart any further. He said, "Well, I just wanted to ask you to pray for me. I really need a job. So that's it." But I felt some depths in this man and felt he had the power to explore his deepest beliefs and hopes. So I asked, "Are you in the area, around the retreat house, sometimes?" Trey said that he was, when he went to AA meetings. So I invited him: "Well, drop in on me some times. Will you?" Trey was plainly pleased: "Sure, I'll give you a call and get a time that's good." He had thought about this before—and was leaving contented.

And that was the first of many sessions of spiritual direction. Sometimes Ignatian directors do the inviting because we recognize a need or a desire that the seeker may not see or does not know how to express.

Touchstones

- This first time, we listen to know whether the seeker will be helped by ongoing direction.

- We learn some things about the seeker's story, their ordinary life, and their prayer.

- We learn whether the seeker lives familiar with God.

- We get a sense of the seeker's religious and the spiritual practices.

- We might make a tentative decision to continue meeting.

- We try to think what will help them leave in peace and joy.

12. Listening Yet Another Time to a Well Known Seeker

We meet with some seekers over some months or years. But each time one comes, we listen as though this were our first conversation.

Of course, we will be remembering some of their earlier experiences. When Donald said that he'd been in a desolation, for instance, his director felt the weight of earlier darknesses. But he was careful to ask, "Do you know what it's about?" He kept their focus on the present experience.

Focused on the present experience of an experienced seeker, we expect to note consolation and desolation. And when these are strong, we expect the seeker to know what they are about. Donald, for instance, knew that a desolation told him to ask himself where he had failed to trust God, and what exactly the failures was about. If he had not explored that, his director would have asked.

Weighing these two spirits, consolation and desolation, assessing their strength and where they might lead, we are opening the basic question: Where has the Spirit been working with this seeker, and where is the Spirit moving them now? We judge more confidently when we can remember earlier experiences. To secure that, a lot of us learned early on to keep notes after each conversation and to refer back to them. Keeping notes takes self-discipline and the practice of prudence and generosity. Not every spiritual director does it, but the practice is necessary when we are first beginning to direct. And it can be crucial later on when seekers' experiences are more extensive or complex than ordinary.

The truth is, all seekers' experiences are extensive and complex enough. As we listen yet another time, we will have heard how a marriage thrives, for instance, or how a major decision is taking shape or working out. We hear how an attachment has developed and what current temptations might be. Above all, we notice where their spiritual growth has been—Donald slowly growing to humbly accept God's love; Janice, as we'll see, learning the graces of the Gifts Examen.

As a seeker recounts current experience, they are likely to give us some indication of where their spiritual progress lies now. It may be, as Donald's was, directly in his relationship with God our Lord. Or it may be in relationships with others, as Janice's was. In a second marriage, she was making progress in basic gratitude to God by happily turning her daily Examen to practicing the Gifts of the Holy Spirit. She told her director that she was getting along wonderfully with both families.

Janice regularly began her conference talking about her prayer. Like most seekers who come regularly, she has long been praying mentally, though she also found consolation and fruit in some devotions: the rosary, hours of adoration, and Morning and Evening Prayer.

Ordinarily, Janice prayed the prayer of consideration, weaving the Word and her world together in the presence of the Lord. During direction, she would be talking about Jesus' experiences and without a jump, be talking about a grandchild. For her prayer is about the discipline she needs in her asceticism of love of all of those He had given her to love.

Her prayer was also about the disciplined asceticism Jesus lived as He did His Father's will. She was well educated and had a master's degree, which helped as she deepened in prayer. She was able to consider, for instance, Jesus' perspective on observing the Sabbath and His perceptions of the way different scribes and Pharisees thought. She was challenged in her own valuing by reflecting on Jesus'. One or other time, it seemed to her director that her imagination was running away with her. But he only rarely had to challenge her to be sure she was praying because she would move from her imagined experience to naming a real need of someone in her life.

Over the months in a long relationship, a director may notice some temptations in any seeker's prayer. Sloth, of course, and the weakness hiding under it, like fear of what the Lord may ask. When a seeker says that "nothing much is happening" in prayer, they may be using prayer as a time for just centering or resting—comfortable chair, fragrant candle, consoling thoughts—which usually ends in a mild desolation. But when "nothing is happening," we do well to probe the need of a conversion of heart in one of the areas of human experience so that they can love and serve God better.

Any desolation in prayer may turn out to be a struggle with a serious lack in the disciplined asceticism of love. Janice went through a desolation after a family gathering. As she told about it, the memory of an unfortunate in-law incident surprised her: "I've never gotten over what they did to me." With some discussion, she realized that the Holy Spirit was challenging her to forgive the offenders from her heart.

As happened with Janice, some incident can move a seeker to look back over their lives and come up against something negative. "I have always regretted sinning that way when I was young." We may have to help seekers carefully distinguish repentance, which engages the seeker and our merciful God, from regret, which engages the seeker alone. Remarks like, "I've been sorry for that every day of my life," point to serious breaches in the disciplined asceticism of love—failures to discipline self-pity and self-absorption. Directors find ways to challenge this immobility.

But in most meetings in a long spiritual direction relationship, we just sit quietly listening to what the seeker wants to tell now about their lives. Mature disciples live consoled by the gifts that Jesus gives us: *my peace I give you* and *joy to the full*. As we listen to them, we follow our principle that the more they tell us, the better we can help them.[80] We learn by God's grace to appreciate this seeker deeply, and to honor their experiences in the Holy Spirit. We keep that Holy Spirit in mind when we discern a time to guide or challenge.

And we live aware that experienced seekers who come to us often make us reflect on ourselves. Their holy experiences might move us to adopt the attitude described by Josiah Royce as "repentant fallibilism," which is at once humble and bold. Begging the Spirit's care, we say simply what we now see, always ready to need to change. So we live accepting our election in grace and live, day by day, joyful lives in Christ, whose love we mean to pass on to other seekers.

Touchstones

- In each conversation, we want to hear what is happening now.

- We note whether they are in consolation or desolation—and ask if we have to.

- We expect to hear about their prayer, and how daily life has woven into it.

- We listen quietly to what the seeker wants to tell about, hoping to discern where the Spirit is leading to progress in love.

13. Listening to a Seeker Met Briefly or Only Once

Ruby (her name came up later) turned to me in the parking lot and said: "Oh, you're the one who gave the prayer last Saturday." She referred to an afternoon of practicing the *lectio divina*. She then explained that she had appreciated the afternoon though "she didn't pray that way," and what she did had helped her for a long time. What I heard this elderly lady ask for was simple: that I agreed that her prayer was "all right," for the Spirit leads each one of us. That was an easy one.

Conversations like this happen in various ways. We make friendly contact when we are standing in line at a store or sitting in a waiting room (hardly happens during a pandemic). And of course, when we give retreats we regularly listen to seekers who have signed up for a brief session of "spiritual direction." Often enough, retreatants present a problem—children not going to Mass or their own struggle to keep the retreat alive all year. Whatever we might suggest, we try to help them see the problem in the light of their ongoing relationship with God in Christ.

But whatever stories we hear, we keep listening to this person, speaking in this moment. We practice a fearless empathy. Sinners ourselves, we are compassionate as our heavenly Father is compassionate—as He gives rain and sunshine without judging and out of love, in the same way, we give attention and concern.[81]

Casual seekers talk with a friendly listener about almost anything. Much of the time, they are glad to find someone who will listen. But one or other hesitantly seek help living the faith or keeping hope strong.

So, first about what we're doing with the ones who just need someone to listen. When we are in a position to do it, we do it generously. We listen to where the seeker thinks they are in the present moment. We unwrap the story they are telling to find where their spirit is now. What in their minds and hearts made them discern that they wanted to tell somebody?

When they tell us about something good, as Ruby did, we find it easy. Basic active listening will bring us to reflect to them what they are saying.

"It sounds like you're happy about that." If there's reason and time to ask, our questions are "open," beginning with *What* or *How* or *Does that seem...*, always helping them see further into what happened or into themselves.

When they have some challenge or problem to talk about, though, we need real discernment. They may need to know whether some habit of thought or feeling or deed is holy or not. Brandon, for instance, remarked that he was not sure that he believed playing golf with some friends was sinful. He wondered out loud whether having his wife oppose this healthy exercise was just "a cross he has to bear." But the way he delivered this thought made it clear that he was fighting his conscience.

Some make it clear that they don't need help, and brief encounters can present us with a seeker who wants to make sure we know that they are comfortable in themselves. Ruby, the lively lady up above, was surely one of those.

It might be that both Ruby and Brandon were only beginning to lead a discerning life. Seekers who are beginning it usually show that they are or are not content with where God has led them at this point. If they are not content, we might be able to help them identify a desolation and ask what it's about. If they are content, we might help them envision spiritual growth. In either case, we encourage them. We want those we encounter to leave us with hope.

The seeker may have a lively sense of how things stand between themselves and God. Ruby surely showed that—she was content with "her way of praying." This kind of contentment can well be a clear sign that the person is trusting God, living today in His presence, and leaving the future to His providence. A holy way of life.

But a lot of times, brief encounters leave us with the sense that this person does not know where they really stand with God. That may be dangerous spiritually, or it may be a grace in the form of a mature spiritual assessment of how they stand on this day. In either case, every beginning seeker needs help being firm in the first great discernment: God lives and loves me, cares for me, and loves me too much to leave me as I am.

It might be that we find it possible to ask whether they would want to meet again. This demands a quick decision, and the swift weighing of a lot of variables: does this person want help, what kind and can I give it, have I time to give it, where and when would we meet?

In Philip's case, that was an easy decision. I knew that he was in a program for making a retreat in daily life. In this brief encounter, I heard a truly mature Christian just want to share the joy of living in Christ. We met in a public place and he was responding to my, "Philip! How's your retreat going?" He could tell about making progress in prayer and learning better how to pray. He was also quite blunt that he didn't know anything about this "discernment thing."

In an instant, my feeling was firm and clear. So I asked him whether he'd like me to try to help him with that. We agreed that he would email me and we'd set up a time and place. That began a long spiritual friendship, a beautiful grace that sometimes the Spirit initiates with a casual meeting.

About the other person in these encounters—the spiritual director—our norm is that the seekers leave with the impression that they have met a mature Christian who is quietly secure, notably compassionate, and clearly joyful. And we directors consider it a consolation that we pray for them for a little while after we've met.

Touchstones

- Casual contacts can be occasions of grace for those we meet.

- We listen to each seeker as though they were as important to me as they are to our Lord.

- We unwrap the stories they tell to find where their mind and heart are now.

- Wherever they stand, we want to help them make progress.

- We may decide to invite them to spiritual direction.

II. THE SECOND LISTEN: AN IGNATIAN SPIRITUAL DIRECTOR

14. The Listening that Makes Spiritual Direction Ignatian

Ignatian spiritual directors listen with our own spirituality in mind, as do all directors. Benedictine, Franciscan, Carmelite will all listen from within their own communities and inner lives. All of us focus on the same thing, of course: the seeker's unique relationship with God. But how we do that differs in two ways.

First, a spiritual director in each tradition enables a characteristic relationship with God. In the monastic tradition like the Benedictine and Carmelite, directors help seekers shape an interior life in a community of seekers on the same quest. The mendicants, led by Dominicans and Franciscans, live in urban priories in poverty to do ministry among the poor.

In Ignatian spirituality, directors enable a relationship with God not in a place or a way of life, but in an *experience*—the *Spiritual Exercises.* These shape distinctive attitudes and commitments, like being called to work with Christ the King, and living to give greater service in whatever way of life. When this unique dialogue with the Lord continues after *Exercises,* seekers are living Ignatian spirituality.

What do we hope to hear when we listen them? An Ignatian director hopes to feel that a seeker maintains the reverent familiarity with God they reached in *Exercises.* We hope that they continue living toward greater love by discerning attachments and shaking off disordered affections that are obstacles to intimacy with the Lord and with others. For familiarity with God flows into all our other relationships, and those loves flow back into our love of God. This is our disciplined asceticism—the ordering of our love for God who is always in action and in Him, the ordering of our love for all the others in our lives.

❖

Spiritual traditions also differ in their characteristic relationship with the world. The monastic way is based on a place, the monastery; the mendicant, on the chosen style of life, truly poor among the urban poor. The Ignatian way of relating to the world takes many different shapes: lay or cleric, scholar or activist, politician or carpenter. But each seeker has a personal role in the world, which no one else can fill, and which the Lord makes known in their personal gifts and desires.

What unites all of this into a coherent spirituality is our decision to engage our life world as Jesus engaged His: to serve it, redeem it lovingly, and transform it into the Kingdom of God. We passionately apply whatever means the Lord supplies—including failure and suffering. Our purpose is to find God always working in all things, from the most intimate in my life to the epochal life of the planet. So this Jesuit pope can ask all of us to work personally,

> to bring the whole human family together to seek a sustainable and integral development, for we know that things can change. The Creator does not abandon us; he never forsakes his loving plan or repents of having created us.[82]

Whatever the seeker's role in the world and however their familiarity with God has developed, the Ignatian director expects to hear activity in all parts of their lives. This means progressing in intimacy with God in prayer, particularly with the Lord Jesus. But also in an engagement with their lifeworld, where God is active: neighborhood, city, parish—even cultural movements in nation and world.

Most importantly, we live intimate with others whom God gives us to love—some necessary relationships, some chosen. They all also grow and change. We are therefore challenged to live our daily lives always discerning the next good thing to do for love of neighbor as well as for

God. Ignatian directors tend to feel it odd that a seeker would never have anything to say about these relationships, especially family and spousal.

These loves thrive in what is done, so as Ignatian directors we listen carefully for signs of Ignatian discernment. Chex—the one who got desolate doing a new kind of prayer—did this discernment when he recognized that what came as a good spirit led to darkness and had to be repudiated. Janice also told me about an important discernment she made after all her children had left her home empty.

She and Chex both lived mindful of the ongoing interaction of thinking, feeling, and doing. This is "mindfulness"—not today's psychological fashion, but a mindfulness shaped in faith and hope. This mindfulness lays the foundation under Ignatian discernment and enables the enactment of our disciplined asceticism of love. This was quite clear in the way Janice handled a family situation.

Janice had settled into a routine of prayer and being grandmother of her daughter's two babies. As the months passed, she could see that her daughter had to get a job. She understood well that her son-in-law's income was not enough for the family—and had let that influence her vote in a recent election. Now, she discerned what love asked her to do.

She told me that she was aware of feeling really disappointed not to be able to enjoy the empty nest freedom a little longer. But she had discerned, disciplined her feelings, and mentioned to her daughter before being asked that she "could watch the children," if that became necessary. It happened. It's worth noting that Janice was given a deep consolation in renewed motherly love and confidence that she was doing God's will.

Hers is the kind of spiritual freedom Ignatian directors listen for. It comes down to hoping to hear a contemplative in action, invited to labor alongside Jesus to build in their own lifeworld the kingdom that is "peaceful, just, and fraternal, and acceptable as an offering to God."[83]

Touchstones

- Each spirituality develops a characteristic relationship with God and with the world.

- In Ignatian spirituality, the characteristic relationship with God is founded in the *experience* of a dynamic a dialogue with God our Lord in the Exercises.

- The Ignatian relationship with the world is Jesus': to serve it, redeem it lovingly, and transform it into the Kingdom of God.

- We expect to witness seekers making progress in their prayer and in the whole of their lives.

- Our "mindfulness" is being aware of the interplay of head, heart, and hand as we discern and practice our disciplined asceticism of love.

- Ignatian directors hope all seekers are progressing as contemplatives in action.

15. Listening with the Disciplined Asceticism of Love in Mind

Until the classical spiritualities developed, the holy yearning had led ascetics to punish themselves, sometimes savagely. One ascetic stared at the sun until he was blind; others imprisoned themselves in tiny cells. But as the great traditions developed, their asceticisms have been *disciplined,* rejecting ancient excesses of treating the body as an enemy of the soul and the world mainly as an occasion of sin.

Current asceticisms are much more positive. Benedictine, Franciscan, Carmelite all guide head, heart, and hands to seeking God, leaving space for creativity. This is easily visible in the disciplined asceticism of a monastery's peaceful, very regular, order of common prayers, works, fasts, and silences.

Ignatian asceticism is not so visible, because it disciplines many styles of life steeped in the world's daily busyness. If we follow an asceticism, what is it? What disciplined asceticism do I expect of myself and what can I realistically expect to hear from other seekers?

The first thing to recognize is that we do live an Ignatian asceticism. It begins when we choose a clear focus for our lives: we put God first and intend to find Him in our daily lives—however the Lord calls us to live. When seekers have begun living this first commitment, they show an ease with themselves, a singleness of heart, a freedom in thinking and doing. They have begun to live mindful and humanly mature lives. Like newlyweds, they still have a lot to work at and to struggle through as they mature in love.

Clearly, this takes discipline. "Discipline" is not some strange pile of ashes held over from the past; discipline is and entirely modern fire. Professional football players order everything to their sport: food and drink, exercise, rest, relationships, and everything else including their thinking. Ballet dancers live stretched in technique and conditioning, and Wall Street lawyers purposely discipline their commutes, meals, leisure activities, and family lives to reach success in sixty- or seventy-hour workweeks. These disciplines taken as a whole coalesce into a kind of secular asceticism.

These heroes put a lot of order into thoughts, desires, and habitual ways of acting to reach their goal.

❖

So do we. We have the greatest of human purposes: to love God above everything and to live serving Him always at work in the world. Unlike our secular ascetics, however, we are not in charge. So our first discipline, as Master Ignatius suggests at the beginning of *Spiritual Exercises,* is to wait for God "with a wide open spirit, generous toward our Creator and Lord, offering to God all our desiring and our freedom to choose."[84]

I have found this real generosity moving many seekers, some matured and still making progress, some not yet tested and maturing. How this maturing goes, the weeks of the *Exercises* suggest. The First Week, Master Ignatius mentions, is like the "Purgative life."[85] We struggle first to free ourselves, or let the Lord free us, from actual sins against love. For some, that means less alcohol or impatience and temper. But it can just as well mean something positive: an exercise routine, time with spouse or with friends, or joining AA. This is the "purgative way," and the mature know that it doesn't end with the retreat.

Then we turn to the "Illuminative way," to learning to know, love, and follow the Lord and everyone and everything in Him. We throw light on attachments and desires. All of us need good, sound convictions, affections and attachments. But even good ones can grow sour and lead us the wrong way. It often comes down to very ordinary things. Jeff, a married man with children, was really attached to beers after work. He quit so he could play with his children and (a good Christmas gift) talk quietly with his wife.

None of us will persevere in these purposeful efforts without regular prayer. This would be our "Unitive way," because we are praying to "find God in all things," and to live united with God working actively in our life world.[86] This is a *sine-qua-non* in Ignatian asceticism: however we live in the world's busyness, we pray daily. It consoles a director to hear a seeker detail time and place and manner of morning prayer and the Examen.

Note that this disciplined asceticism can be done well or slothfully, generously or stingily. We tend to hope that each seeker will do *more,* led by the Spirit. But we keep aware that a sound principle is to counsel no more than a seeker can at this time manage. A wide range of seekers are invited by *Spiritual Exercises* to embrace Ignatian spirituality, and have done it from the start. Master Ignatius and the early Jesuits offered *Exercises* to the illiterate in the plaza and to the masters of Paris, to the saintly to the corrupt, the tepid to the heroic.

Just now in our nation's story, we are offering them to many who *seek only some instruction and peace of heart.*[87] But we are not surprised to hear a seeker who quietly rejoices in the interchange of gifts with God our Creator and Lord, whose prayer focuses not on self, but on God in Christ and on those whom God gives them to love and to serve.

All of this belongs in an Ignatian spiritual director's way of listening—our own minds and hearts shaped by the disciplined asceticism of love of God and neighbor.

Touchstones

- All spiritualities follow a disciplined asceticism according to their chosen purposes and contexts.

- Many outstanding professionals follow a kind of secular disciplined asceticism in seeking their success.

- Our first discipline is to wait for the Spirit with open and generous hearts.

- Ignatian asceticism orders head, heart, and hands to our purpose of finding God in everything and serving Him in love.

- The discipline we follow is for love of God and the others in our lives, and our own selves.

- The discipline starts with daily prayer and the Examen.

- A seeker's way of living this disciplined asceticism can be magnanimous, generous, or just adequate.

16. The Deeper Purpose of a Seeker's First Visit

A seeker coming to direction for the first time will usually tell why they have come. But the Holy Spirit may have a different purpose in mind. Cecil, for instance, a forty-something lawyer, came to "learn more about Ignatian spirituality" and ended up learning some things about himself that were surprising and encouraging. Ignatian directors listen in the conviction that the Holy Spirit is always inspiring and guiding.

New seekers will tell us any of a wide range of purposes and hopes. These run from a current vexing problem—in prayer, in marriage, in depression—to discerning what a not-yet-focused desire "to do God's will" might mean. Whatever the seeker's concrete purpose, we frame it in the larger Ignatian purpose: the greater glory of God. They may just want to solve a problem. We always want something more, convinced that "they will make progress in all spiritual concerns only as far as they have set aside their self-love, self-will, and self-interest."[88]

And as their purposes differ, so do their spirits. We may face the task of helping them accept that God is with them and attends to them constantly. *Do you not know that you are God's temple and that God's Spirit dwells in you?*[89] We find out that some have not yet caught the fire of that good news, and we may have to challenge, or encourage, or even exhort.

But we are correct to listen with this presumption in mind: that the person I am listening to for the first time has been freed from *the law of sin and death,* and now seeks to find what infinite Love is doing in their life.[90] So as we listen to the story about their present situation, we want to hear whether their recent days have been lived in consolation or not. If they have not, we know we need help them know why. If they have lived with lively hope and faith, we try to assess how open and generous they are.

Their generosity might not show immediately. Trey, for instance—the seeker who had lost his job—came to see me as the retreat director for a very mundane purpose: he needed prayers for a job. But as I listened to him, the man's openness and his plain love for God and for his three daughters moved me. A certain largeness of spirit—generosity—emerged. Trey's was not a disciplined and orderly mind. But when I asked whether he'd want to continue in spiritual direction, his face lit up in surprise and delight. He knew he was close to God but never thought of himself as a candidate for spiritual direction.

I thought he was. Our relationship was not neat. It eventually turned into something closer to a holy friendship—a traditional development deep in the way of proceeding that was started by a group of "friends in the Lord."[91]

This is where the Ignatian disciplined asceticism of love for neighbor leads, by the grace of God. Spiritual friendship is the Holy Spirit's gift to seekers who are free enough to enjoy it and to maintain the balance between director and seeker.

❖

Beverly had that gift of spiritual friendship. She belonged to a bible-reading group of friends in the Lord who had been meeting for some years, listening to one another with affection and concern. Beverly phoned one day asking "for spiritual direction." She wanted to get beyond just studying the bible.

As soon as we traded names and a very little more, Beverly explained that she prays the *lectio divina* that they had found on the web. She is just not sure she "does it right." As she explained it, Beverly was using the classic *lectio divina* drawn from the monastic way of life: read, meditate, pray, contemplate. It was this final dynamic, *contemplate,* that stumped her. "I don't quite know what to do with it....what it has to do with anything."

The monastic *lectio,* done fully, ends in *contemplation.* But when Beverly's prayer time ended, she flew into a dozen pieces of busyness that seem to have gone untouched in her prayer. An Ignatian adaptation in the *lectio* responds precisely to this. Its movements are: read, consider, pray, discern. The prayer of *consideration* weaves together Jesus' human experience and my own human experience: Word and world. Then we stand ready to *discern,* and face the busyness that we have considered in our prayer. This is the purpose of Ignatian prayer even during the *Spiritual Exercises.*[92]

I explained this briefly to Beverly—it's fairly easy to grasp. Then, as a director, I was tempted to continue with the practical theology behind the change: about our busy God and how we are co-creating our lifeworld. But that would have been moving ahead of Beverly, whom the Spirit was moving with a desire to go further into prayer. To what end would have to emerge in time.

This situation is common. The director can see that the seeker's own spirit is moving, but where and for what is not yet clear. As we listen, we are likely to think of good suggestions to make. But the Ignatian director prefers to wait for the seeker to find for themselves where the Spirit is leading them.

So as Trey and I had done, Beverly and I set a time for another meeting.

Touchstones.

- Seekers come for their own purpose; the Holy Spirit may have brought them for a different one.

- We are correct to presume we face a disciple of Christ but we have to find out whether they know they are sinners loved.

- We are quicker to keep seeing a seeker who has a generous, open spirit.

- Seekers come for their purpose; the Holy Spirit may have a different one.

- We urge the *lectio divina* that moves through consideration to discernment.

- Convinced that the Spirit is guiding this seeker, we choose not to make suggestions quickly, but to wait for them to find their way.

17. Listening to Someone Who Lives Ignatian Spirituality

Listening to a seeker who has lived Ignatian spirituality for a while allows more promptly going deeper into their experience and its meanings. Rebecca, for instance, prayed through a serious discernment whether to apply to be director of a Catholic institution. Her director could trust that she appreciated the significance of desolations and consolations.

And we can expect that they want to deepen their relationship with God and with others—what we think of as "making progress." Occasionally, though, an experienced seeker thinks they need "to pray better." We listen carefully to that, because our egotism often shades that desire less to the greater glory of God and more to the greater consolation of His friend. It's a common temptation among the more experienced.

And it was the problem—praying better—that Chex needed to talk about in his next session. Chex (his surname ran on to several more thorny syllables) was a retired businessman who made retreats regularly and prayed a longer while every day. He read a lot and belonged to a small group of friends in the Lord who met, prayed, and shared together. He had come to see me intermittently over some years. Now he phoned with a problem he didn't remember having had before.

It was his prayer. He was confused and lost in his prayer—distracted and somehow aimless. He had been desolate before but never like this. He was deeply confused. He explained that he was trying a new form of prayer, following the instructions in a book a friend had urged him to get into. I had heard of neither the book's author nor the form of prayer it was promoting. As Chex tried to describe it, he kept going back to his own desolation. He did not understand it. It was like total emptiness. He had never had this long a period when his prayer was so empty.

Chex paused and I said: "Let me ask you something, Chex. Can you tell when the desolation began?" Chex looked up and said that it started about when he got the book and started trying this new kind of prayer. Understanding lit his face. "Oh, of course. The book. The 'new' kind of prayer."[93]

Chex had quickly applied the Ignatian principle: What looks like a good idea leading to grace can turn out to be no such thing; "a bad angel assumes the form of an angel of light."[94] The book and his friend's strong endorsement seemed to promise progress in prayer; it ended in confusion.

Chex would also have to apply another Ignatian principle: When we are in a desolation, we never change a decision, but "it helps to change *myself* against the desolation."[95] He knew he had to go back to praying the way the Lord had led him. But this desolation taught him something further: he also had to change *himself.* He had lunged into this "new prayer" because he was attached to the comfort and peace that prayer brought him and wanted more of it. The Lord will not abide that insult.

Our prayer is not an instrument that we can improve on or a performance we can make more perfect. Changing from his long-held practice of prayer to this book's "new form" felt to Chex like moving up from an old fiddle to a Stradivarius violin. God mercifully taught him that even when we feel like an old upright piano, the Spirit draws harmonies from us in this communion of two infinitely unequal, freely loving, wills.

❖

All of us can grow attached to what is good—even, like Chex, to the good of praying regularly. Sister Rose's experience was with a good attachment to a good ministry. A woman of about fifty, quick-witted and talented in public affairs, her daily prayer had the harmony of deep and long-established communion of freedom with God. She was a member of one of the several congregations founded on Ignatian spirituality.[96] She understood and practiced discernment and had had to practice it as her congregation changed after the Second Vatican Council.

Rose came to talk about a change she was asked to consider. She needed to discern whether to accept a call to join the central administration of her congregation or to remain in her fruitful ministry at the university. Her discernment proved difficult because the fruits of each ministry were great though quite different. Complicating it was the reality that she did not feel sure of her gifts of administration and leadership.

As we met regularly over the next several months, Rose went through several periods of consolation and desolation. The director's work throughout was to keep her focused on the main issues of freedom: attachment to her ministry and generosity with God. She had to weigh the depth and sources of her attachment to the ministry she would be leaving. She also had to challenge her feelings about gifts she had that had never been really tested—a point I had to draw her back more than once. Many others who knew her well saw some leadership gifts in her; these, she had to pray to accept.

Rose made her decision on the grounds of the greater good and joined the leadership of her congregation. She was content, though she grieved a while, missing the university students' concerns and the joyful daily contacts. Even great spiritual indifference like hers does not exempt us from nature's laws of growth in the kingdom of earth: we get attached to its wonderful good things.

This soil is where both good attachments and holy magnanimity grow—and where directors spend most time with seekers who live Ignatian spirituality.

Touchstones

- We see prayer not as an instrument that we use to communicate with God, but as a dialogue and communion initiated by our infinitely free God.

- We are aware that praying regularly can become more a human comfort and security than a free and generous dialogue with God our Lord.

- We keep aware of how what looks good and holy can lead to what is not [332 and 333].

- Our discernments can be problematic when we have not accepted openheartedly the concrete gifts God has given and still gives to us.

- Discernments among mature disciples and seekers are commonly about being led from one good to a greater good.

18. Ignatian Listening in Casual or Brief Encounters

Why does it matter that we are Ignatian directors when we have a casual or brief contact? Fifteen minutes of counsel during a weekend retreat, over coffee at a conference, waiting in a line—what difference can it make? We need to think about it, because the Holy Spirit uses even a shared cup to bring people alive.

We should go right to the two sources of why it matters: people's needs and people's desires. As Rachel remarked about her two-week cruise in the Caribbean: "People are dry and thirsty," and they usually react eagerly to someone who offers them the living water of hope.

Rachel, to go back to her experience, is a very experienced Ignatian director and teacher. After a day or two, she started feeling that *everyone* wanted to talk. Fortunately, she admitted, the scenery gave God glory and she had time to contemplate it. She needed it because casual contacts like the ones she was having take energy.

We want to attend to the person facing me for a little while as though we had nothing else to do. The people we encounter even briefly ought to sense that we are truly interested in them. They will if our interest is in this *person*, not in some *individual* we happened to meet. This person is dear to God our Creator and has been redeemed by Jesus Christ. Do they know to live that in peace and joy?

If that's how we live, ourselves, we will be a joy to meet even casually. Occasionally, we find ourselves in a conversation deeper than the weather report. We find ourselves in seminars and workshops standing with people we do not know. We can decide: just share names and chat, or show interest in this person. What brought them here? Have they done seminars before? What did you make of the last talk? Our conversation shows what we, ourselves, are really interested in and care about. It can be a joy to meet with such people in our parishes, at social affairs, or even waiting in line in a grocery store. Casual encounters remind us to live so that we are a joy to meet, even briefly.

Somehow, religion or spirituality come up—or we bring it up. Brandon, for instance, wore a golf glove and as we waited to pay for our purchases, I smiled and said, "Golf." He answered, "Yeah, my religion." By the time both of us checked out—very slow line—Brandon had exposed a set of attachments that needed attention: to golf, to his golf partners, to neglecting the attention his wife and family needed. He was clearly wound-up and a bit tense. "Golf was his religion." As we parted, I quipped that living at par with his family would last longer than reaching par on the golf course. He laughed. A little.

We sometimes casually meet someone living in an Ignatian context, like a member of the Christian Life Community.[97] These men and women form small groups that pray and work together. They make the 18th or the 19th annotation retreat and may offer to guide others through them. Asking about their spiritual activities and showing understanding is a good way of *encouraging one another,* which St. Paul urged.[98] Meeting with them often leaves the sense of meeting with Pope Francis's "middle-class holiness," and the encounter itself can be a joy.

Another place for brief encounters is the weekend-retreat. Men and women formed for the ministry now give the retreat talks in houses all over the country. During them, we then find ourselves meeting with retreatants in brief time-slots. Experience suggests that these are usually pastoral counsel rather than spiritual direction. For they commonly have to do with a difficulty, a problem, or a suffering. Older parents are pained that their children do not go to Mass. An older man wanted to know whether he would go to hell if he had his body cremated. A devout young woman asked about a book.

We listen to each person to hear whether the seeker already knows what they've asked, like the parish staffer who asked whether she sinned by not confessing monthly. "Well, what do you think?, either confirms their own consciences or creates occasion for some catechesis. If they don't know—like the father who was not sure whether he had sinned by visiting a relative in a home instead of going to the only available Mass—we answer as simply as we know how as mature members of the Church. We humbly accept that this seeker wants *my* thoughts, not the pope's.

We are wise to be alert to people who have an initial interest in spirituality. We catch the "sign of the times" that mature lay men and women are "dry and thirsty," eager to find credible witnessing to God and hope. So are mature disciples in the various denominations. Directors in Dallas' Ignatian Spirituality Institute regularly face Christians, including clergy, who are not Catholics. So it is everywhere: "People are dry and thirsty." For us, that is not a problem; it is an opportunity.

❖

How can we describe the Ignatian director's mindset in casual encounters?

First, we respect this person and we want to listen to them. This is a basic norm in the disciplined asceticism of love for our neighbor: we *listen to each other.* Then, we can encourage them to go on by using active listening techniques like reflecting back to them what they have said. To Brandon, for instance: "So the golf links are your cathedral?" Then they are likely to go on, which is what we want.

As they tell their story, we hope to hear a yearning to *know the Lord,* however inchoate. They may talk about a concrete grace of believing or a struggle with faith. Then we wait for an opening to share what we believe. We will solve no problems, but we can give witness, *always with courtesy and respect and with a clear conscience,* as one director did by quietly telling a seeker that he, too, had once lost his faith.[99]

We are ready to say about their experience, "That sounds really good to me." For we are more inclined to admire their good actions and thank God for their graces than to venture advising and guiding them. The reality is that casual encounters tend to be open-ended and rarely leave us content with a success.

We might close them as we walk away by praying for the person we've just left in God's hands.

Touchstones

- In casual encounters, we face a person dear to God in Christ and give them our focused attention.

- If faith and hope in God do not come up, we are glad to snatch a chance to bring them up courteously and honestly.

- We want to confirm others in their faith and hope; but we are ready to give witness.

- When a seeker mentions being in a crisis, we think of it not as a problem but as an opportunity to make progress in Christ.

19. Making Progress, Ongoing Conversion, and the Five Realms of Experience

Shaun has reached a hard place. He is a hard-working man but attends daily Mass at the downtown cathedral with lots of workers and laborers. He prays a while daily and visits his spiritual director. But he is plagued by his harsh judgments about minorities and "the free-loaders." He has been perplexed, believing in each person's dignity but unable to acknowledge it in many, many cases.

Then one morning he was standing in the slow line to receive Communion—corona-virus, six-foot social distancing, and masks. He found himself thinking about receiving Communion with people who are probably on food stamps, liberals, racists, etc. Then, he told his director, a thought just stopped him dead: "And I'm standing with them." It was a light and a grace: he suddenly knew in his heart that he *was* one of "them."

His director saw this as a religious conversion—a change of heart toward being *perfect as your Father is perfect.*[100] She remarked, "This was a great grace, Shaun." Before it, he was judging people; now, like God *who makes the sun shine on the evil and on the good, and sends rain on the just and on the unjust,* Shaun was letting his love reach out to all around him. Shaun said he really felt like a different man now. But in a fit of realism he added, "But it'll take a while."

It will, of course; a conversion has to set us to developing new habits of thought, feeling, and action—it takes a while.[101] The breakthrough at Communion opened a way for him to progress where he needs it in the disciplined asceticism of love of God and neighbor and self. Like all seekers, Shaun will naturally meet some crises as he works out his new mindset and heartset.

When we listen to a seeker tell about a crisis, we might both feel that it's a set-back in their life. But our norm is to face a crisis not as a problem, but as an opportunity. For the all-wise Spirit is still guiding the seeker, and we are serious about this principle: *We know that all things work together for good for those who love God, who are called according to his purpose.*[102] The crisis can be personal health or a bad business break. It can be a grave problem like a spouse's cancer or even a crisis of faith tested by a secular ideology.

When Ignatian directors listen to experiences like any of these, our expectation is that the Spirit is opening a way for this seeker to make progress. We are not doing therapy and we want to get beyond just offering spiritual comfort—though that may be all a seeker will listen to for now. We are listening to see if we can help this seeker discern what progress the Lord is calling them to.

Discerning this might be more secure if we interpret the experience as principally affective, intellectual, religious, moral, or social-political. An experience engages our whole person, of course: head, heart, and hands. But ordinarily, the experience lights up (like Shaun's) or darkens one of the principal realms, and looking deeper into that realm will open the whole experience.

Shaun's conversion, for instance, falls in the realm of the religious. He had not thought that prejudicial thinking about others had anything to do with his relationship with God in Christ. Then one day this prejudice tainted the perfection of the Communion he received—even as he stood with *them.* The grace meant taking responsibility for his thoughts and feelings toward his fellow citizens, a responsibility he would have to take in all Communions to come and in all of his daily living.

Ongoing conversion is the process of constantly taking more mature responsibility for the way we think and feel and act. Shaun's crisis was in his religious experience, though he had some work to do in his affective (those negative feelings) and intellectual life, too. Other stores we've encountered began in other realms of experience.

Some begin with a moral decision. For instance, the father of daughters in their late teens, whose mother was ill, was tempted to omit his morning prayer to prepare breakfast for them. Was frying pancakes a moral obligation? Well, a little reflection with his director—I thought the question as odd as it sounds--turned the question to what the daughters needed and wanted and then to their father's relationship with them. Was his love for them still for "his little girls"? Or had his love for them matured as they were maturing into young women? He discerned that witnessing to them a disciplined asceticism of love was a good way to love them now. Saying his morning prayer and then joining them was a better way to father them than fussing about breakfast.

Sometimes a seeker faces a mainly intellectual challenge. Beverly, whose *lectio divina* got her nowhere, had to understand the difference between bible study and praying with the gospels. But this clearer understanding quickly changed her daily prayer on Jesus' human experience—clearly a religious matter, and hugely enriched them, an affective matter in her heart.

At times in our spiritual lives, the Holy Spirit nudges us, leaving us lonesome and fending for ourselves without Her help.[103] It's when we begin to notice that we are lonesome for God that we are likely to find in one of the realms of our experience the way to keep making progress in this disciplined asceticism of love of God and neighbor—and, guided by Jesus Christ—love of self.

Ignatian spirituality is sometimes called "heady." Well, it is—at least, to the extent that our discernment entails our head as well as our heart and hands. And sometimes, it's easier to see what's happening when a seeker's experience opens first in one or other realm of human experience: intellectual, affective, moral, religious, and social-political. Through it, we might get to the heart of the matter. And when we're listening, to the heart of the seeker, too.

Touchstones

- Our human experiences might come as intellectual, moral, religious, affective, or social-political—the principal areas of human life.

- Our ongoing conversion can be provoked by the Spirit in any of these areas.

- We experience as whole persons—head, heart, and hand—and the areas overlap and interact.

- Ignatian directors listen to seekers' stories with these realms of experience in mind.

- Looking into an experience through any one of them helps open the meaning of the whole experience.

III. THE THIRD LISTEN
THE OTHER SEEKER IN THE ROOM

20. I Listen to My Self

The third listen requires being aware not of the seeker, but of the other person in the room. For the seeker has chosen as spiritual guide—*me*, a person who am also a seeker. And I have chosen to listen to them, humbly caring and ready to summon up for their good all the wisdom and knowledge the Spirit has graced me with. So with God's help, I come to our conversation fully self-aware and as wide-awake as my disciplined asceticism can keep me.

Though what Master Ignatius calls "my concerns" will fill my daily colloquies with the Lord, I do not let any of them blur the focus of my attention on the seeker who comes to me.[104] I am ready to be called on—full of empathy and compassion, wisdom and knowledge, and largely content with the concrete particulars of where the Lord has brought me.

To be practical, we might just note some obvious things. Before beginning any conversation, for instance, I have satisfied myself that time and place have worked out, or been explained. I will have generously set aside any busyness, including turning off the phone. Perhaps with that gesture, I have set aside for the moment concerns that will occupy the rest of my day. I may have prayerfully left in God's hands some incomplete projects: trivial ones like gas for the car, more serious ones like waiting for the report of a medical test.

But before taking care of these particular concerns, a mature spiritual director will be aware whether I am in consolation or am being tested in some way. My Examens and my daily prayer keep me aware of where the Spirit is leading me just now. If I cannot keep aware of the Spirit in my own life, I am not likely to be prepared to hear Her working in any other seeker's.

Somehow, it was the Spirit's work that brought me to be listening as a spiritual director. So it's useful to recall sometimes how this happened in my case. It may be that people have just talked to me most of my life. That happens: one director said that when he was in prep school, other boys, even some he did not know well at all, would tell him intimate things about themselves and their families, uninvited. He must have shown the characteristics of a good listener, discreet about what he has heard.

Or he may have had the charism given some. St. Paul lists *wisdom and knowledge* among the Spirit's gifts, and *the ability to distinguish between spirits.*[105] These charisms, the Church has long recognized, are poured into every person baptized in Christ.[106] But St. Paul points out that the Spirit has been particularly generous with some. A young priest's companions used to say of him: "Tell Callaghan. He'll listen to anything." And Callaghan matured into one of those directors to whom people keep going.

Finally, some are now directors because the Spirit drew them to a training program, or to hand it on after making Spiritual Exercises in Daily Life. Often enough at the end of the program or the retreat, some are invited to help on their staffs. We all learn promptly that a truly thorough "training" is actually a formation that reaches every part of our self and life. As we continue, ourselves, to "make progress," we learn that we have to watch that the seekers who come to us also keeping making progress. Those who do not may be being "spiritual" because it's comfortable and re-assuring in this chaos. The Spirit will not let them continue long.

❖

However we have come to be spiritual directors, it will help humility and courage both to keep conscious that we belong to a great spiritual community. The first Community is the Church—we have come into an ancient ministry of the Church and we stand in the line of hermits, abbesses, and monks that reaches back past Madeleine Sophie Barat, Mary Ward, Ignatius, and Benedict to the early desert fathers and mothers.

Currently, we belong to a global Ignatius community of thousands in Bombay, Cape Town, Madrid, Buenos Aires, and many other places on the globe. We may be blessed to be in a local Ignatius cohort like some that have been active for decades: the Ignatius Spirituality Program of Denver, Spiritual Exercises in Everyday Life in Puget Sound, and BRIDGES in St. Louis.

Every member of these Ignatius cohorts retreats daily into our I-self to reflect and pray. We beg the grace to know our Lord Jesus better, to love Him more intimately, and to find in Him the virtues, powers, and authorities to help us grow more like Him. No sensible director would fail to discipline our daily lives to have time each day to be alone with God and with His Word. And the wise have a director of their own.

Accepting the invitation to give spiritual direction may seem like an honor. It surely is that. But it is even more a serious commitment to live as a mature adult visibly united with Christ. "Allow the Spirit to forge in you the personal mystery that can reflect Jesus Christ in today's world."[107] Pope Francis urged this on every mature Christian, but surely it pertains especially to us who give spiritual direction.

We are allowing the Spirit to shape us not as spiritual therapists or as teachers, but as witnesses to Jesus Christ. The Spirit hollows out a space in us to make room for others' free choices and actions. We calmly allow how the Spirit might lead them, and quietly appreciate the special graces they are given.[108]

If we are authentically Ignatius spiritual directors, we give witness of an authentically mature life in Christ. The surest sign of this is that we are on fire and want to pass on the fire. It is not a set of doctrines or practices, but the fire of love for Christ in my heart.

Touchstones

- Listening to another seeker, I am aware that I am, myself, a seeker.
- Some mature disciples have the human characteristics that make good listeners.
- Being mindful of a worldwide community of directors helps us to be humble and courageous.
- Every serious spiritual director habitually carves out daily time for prayer, growing in love with the Lord.

- A wise director has a spiritual director, too.

- We are witnesses, seeking the grace of a Christian character that reflects Christ into our life world.

21. The Gift of Spiritual Direction: A Mentor's Witness

What do I mean when I say that I listen to myself as an Ignatius spiritual director? Carol Atwell Ackels, who gives direction and directs a program to form others, answered this way.

In a recent conversation among directors at a Jesuit retreat house, most agreed with the remark that "I park myself at the door when I go into a room to give direction." They surely meant some common-sense things by that. But I don't think it's a good way to begin thinking seriously about the listener in spiritual direction. The matter is much subtler than "parking myself at the door."

To begin with, we are convinced that the ministry of spiritual direction in the Ignatius tradition is a gift given by God to some among Christ's mature lay disciples. It is a charism, what St. Paul describes as gift, service, and activity—*the manifestation of the Spirit for the common good.*[109] He lists wisdom, knowledge, and discernment—powers and authorities given to Christ's people not only for themselves, but for contributing to the common good of God's holy people.

Among the earliest Jesuits, Pierre Favre had this charism; he seemed to have been born to offer what he called "spiritual friendship." It shaped his life and his self: he was a notably humble man and profoundly prayerful. As Pope Francis noted when preparing to canonize Father Favre, he was always discerning. He would not debate but was always truly open and steadfast in discussion—a man who listened deeply and selflessly.

Whatever gifts and experiences brought us to offer spiritual direction, we consider it an apostolic work and a gift from God—far from just "what some friends are doing." It comes to permeate and energize the way I think, what I feel, and what I do—in good measure, my own interior life. Other seekers' stories sometimes throw startling light on my own life story.

And they often make me surprised that I am given this gift. For I know myself as sinner and selfish. This is a very common experience, the reason every one of us has to weigh our desire to go into this ministry. We continue to pray steadily that the desire I have to listen to and serve others comes from the Lord laboring for those He loves—me and those with whom I journey. We are clear that we are helping the Holy Spirit guide them, knowing that we need help to be sure that the Spirit is guiding us, too.

From the start of our practice, when we listen to ourselves as Ignatius spiritual directors, we are listening particularly to this gift that has been placed by the Lord into lives—both interiorly in my own mind and heart, and exteriorly in the movements in the two kingdoms which have brought many Christians to become seekers. And when we begin listening, we all have to rely heavily on the gift, trusting entirely that this is, indeed, the Lord's work.

When I started, I knew trusting God was the only option, for I knew from the start how very little we have to offer. We are like the little child with enough athletic ability to hit or catch a ball—occasionally. But over time, the gift is shaped and formed—primarily through prayer and experience. But study is important, too, and we have to add reading, retreats, workshops for skill development, mentoring, community with other companions, and meeting with my own spiritual director.

After some time, we are more mature as directors—that's to be expected. Again, staying with the athletic example, we grow more like the college (if not the pro) athlete, who work with their coaches, do the physical and mental training, study the skills of the sport, watch game films, and so forth. And in the end, they can depend on their shaped and developed gift of athleticism to play the sport to the best of their ability. They play with their whole self—always relying on their athletic gift. It gets to be this way as we mature as spiritual directors, integrating experiences and skills with the spiritual gift we began with.

The metaphor goes only so far, it is true. Still, when we have matured as directors, we are aware that we are listening differently because we have grown different, shaped and formed by the spiritual experiences of the gift given to us. We try to remain deeply aware that we are privileged to carry within us a gift to offer to the precious person, beloved of God, who sits across from me. We are aware that gift is given to *me* for *us*, and is enlarged and made greater only when given others.

As the spiritual conversations go on, we stay sensitive to our interior movements: the scriptures that come to mind, and the experiences— Jesus', my own, and the experiences of others I have listened to. I am attentive to how I respond to what the other says, and what my own interior voice says—perhaps about what might be *more* or *better* for this person. I do what I can to determine whether I am reacting or responding.[110] The questions always at the forefront are: Where do I see or hear the Lord; and What will help this person with what I see or hear?

What I mean when I listen to myself, ultimately, is that I rest grateful and content with the gift of spiritual direction given me. It has been shaped and formed by the Lord and by those with whom I journey.

Touchstones

- Being asked to listen to one of Christ's disciples is a gift—to both.

- This gift permeates my thinking, evaluating, and what I am doing; it helps shape my own interior life.

- When we begin giving direction, we rely humbly on the Spirit—and keep on relying as our gift develops.

- This gift develops with effort, like an athletic talent, but always remains a gift.

- We pray and discern and also read, confer, and keep in touch with colleagues.

- And no, we do not "park ourselves at the door" when going in to give direction.

22. The Spiritual Life of the Director

We called on Gustav Mahler's remark about not worshiping ashes but handing on fire. For God has saved us from the vague "spirituality" rampant in our culture just now. We are correct to believe that God intended our spiritual search to belong to Ignatius spirituality.

"Every spiritual search is guided by a particular literature, practice, and community of faith."[111] Our particular literature begins with the book of *Spiritual Exercises;* our practice follows the Ignatius way of proceeding; and our community is, first, the Church and then our Ignatius community.

Those who made the *Spiritual Exercises* generously and with an open heart, all the way to the "Contemplation for Love," have *experienced the fire.* We have left the ashes of sin or of a search for "my authentic self," and accepted the fire of God's love. Then we may have learned, as Master Ignatius believed, that:

> ... when persons go out of themselves and enter into their Creator and Lord, they enjoy continuous instruction, attention, and consolation; they are aware of how the fullness of our eternal Good dwells in all created things, giving them being, and keeping them in existence with His infinite being and presence."[112]

This "awareness" of the Presence of God is not sensing a divine fragrance, but feeling an infinite force of love at every single minute creating me to His liking and shaping events around me so they invite me to accept His providence. This "continuous instruction, attention, and consolation" that God gjves to me moves through words and feelings to what is *done.*[113]

What is done, on my part, is keeping His Commandments and accepting the *musts* His Spirit confronts me with at every stage of my life. It happened to Jesus, who frequently said to His close friends that He *must* do something-- *go to the other towns—be handed over*—and finally, *rise again.*

Beyond the Commandments and *musts,* our Maker leaves us free to desire and choose among all the good things that earth offers us. They are so good, we know, that we become attached to people and things and even to ideas and convictions. So when a seeker struggles to find "God's will," we know intimately how an attachment to a creature can tear at my fragile attachment to God. Then we practice generous self-discipline.

❖

This is the tradition handed on to us. It is not a theory; people actually live this disciplined asceticism of love of God and neighbor and self. We embrace it with God's gifts, including the gifts of *wisdom* and *courage, compassion* and *understanding* that inform our gift of giving spiritual direction. So we keep reading and studying and praying. And with God's help, we remain loyal to a holy cohort.

For us, the first study of all continues to be *Spiritual Exercises,* a text we steadily go back to. We go back to this text not like consulting a handbook full of data and facts. We go back to it because it narrates the inner dynamic of one proven way of dialoguing with God our Lord. Its norms and rules guide the workings of a self intent on being generously open to God and of some of God's initiatives and responses to those who seek Him in this way. It grounds us in our community of faith.

Ignatius communities dot our landscape in retreat houses, spirituality centers, and parishes. Thousands of men and women have made silent weekend Ignatius retreats annually, learning as we did how to experience God in our lives. Many more thousands have made *Exercises in Daily Life.* And colleagues have established open programs to keep us going.

The Office of Ignatius Spirituality on the East coast, for instance, gathers scores of men and women on four weekends during a year and a half to introduce them to Ignatius spirituality. Programs in Chicago and Atlanta, Omaha and Boston, Seattle and New Orleans, began in the 1980s guiding thousands through the *Spiritual Exercises in Daily Life* and forming guides to pass it on. These are easy to find on the web.

Also easy to find is the history of this *reaching out,* this *handing on the fire,* because it has been immensely consequential. Francis Xavier reached out to the Indies and baptized tens of thousands in Christ. Matteo Ricci (+1610) inculturated deeply in China and began bringing its grand culture to Christ. Reaching out moved women like Ven. Mary Ward (+1645) to create a new way of religious life for women in open ministry.[114] It drove St. Rose Philippine Duchesne (+1852) to live improbably in a log cabin on the American western frontier, catechizing child and adult. And in El Salvador in our day, *reaching out* moved Rutilio Grande (+1977) out of the classroom to journey among the people to martyrdom.

This is the spirituality we have made our own. As it has traditionally done, it is moving us to reach out and pass on the way God has given to us. In reality, *the love of Christ urges us on,* and that love we pass on by crossing the threshold from prayer into our ministry and witnessing love's vitality and urgency.[115]

Touchstones

- Any wise search for God will be guided by an established wisdom, practice, and community of faith.

- The full grace of *Spiritual Exercises* brings a continual union with God our Lord constantly creating, and tending us—ongoing consolation.

- Beyond keeping the Commandments and living our *musts,* we reject disordered attachments and discern God's will in the next good thing to do.

- The Ignatius tradition has moved women and men to heroic lives in handing on the fire.

- Each of us benefits from the long historical line of men and women handing on this disciplined asceticism of love; and now, it is our turn.

23. Humbly Living this Disciplined Asceticism

No mature disciple has to make *Spiritual Exercises* to find out that we are sinners. In the Exercises, rather, we learn how we are to live humbly and joyfully as redeemed sinners. This means accepting with our whole hearts how our All Holy God has decided to reconcile Himself to us and then to give us a work to do that will be pleasing to Him.

As we mature in our spiritual lives, we discover that accepting God's forgiveness is the last step in true repentance. It isn't enough to say "I'm sorry" and to determine not to do it again. We have be aware that Jesus told us to *repent* and also to *believe the good news.* This *good news,* we learn, is that we are sent *as we are,* sinful, flawed, and failing, even to offer spiritual direction. This is not our doing: *It is God who, for His own generous purpose, gives you the intention and the power to act.*[116]

When we repent honestly and wholly, we will arrive astonished to the indescribable tenderness of God's justice and mercy, both. For it may be that, as we needed law to begin to understand how our creature's actions can be sins against the holy God, so we need His mercy to appreciate how His love encompasses both the goodness He has forged in us and the sins we find it unfeasible to escape.

For we are still people with one foot in the kingdom of heaven and one still in the kingdom of earth. Our American culture has not proven very successful in dealing with our faults and flaws. We seem to need university research institutes to convince us of what really makes us unhappy.[117] And we Christians, like everyone else, live day after day *dissed*—distracted by the media, disillusioned with our culture, distressed with pederasty in the Church, disappointed with our young, discouraged by bitter political divisions, and a dozen more *disses.* Yet even the more mature among us do not think to consider living dissed as a spiritual condition—a mild, nagging desolation.[118]

Yet, living dissed has everything to do with a lack of deep gratitude to God for what we are and have. Ingratitude is sinful and brings on spiritual desolation. Acting grateful is our way out of this—precisely, being happy with who we are and what we have and then working generously with the gifts God has given us.

When we make progress practicing the gifts we need as we deal with our current challenges, we are working with God, co-creating our selves and our lifeworld at the same time. This, precisely, is what we mean by "finding God in all things." Problems at work, tensions in our families, burdens from those around us in need, listening to another seeker—in all of these contexts, we can experience our loving God. By His gracious gift, we can come to appreciate "how, according to His divine plan, it is the Lord's wish, as far as He is able, to give me Himself."[119] And our joy will be full.

❖

Even so, *we have this treasure in earthen vessels, to show that the transcendent power belongs to God and not to us.*[120] What belongs to us is faltering and failing. I don't mean the deadly sins like blasphemy or adultery—that's a whole other topic. Here, I mean the serious faults and failing that plague us all: flashes of anger, trusting my control and not God's fidelity, harshly judging others, and the rest of it. These failures are hard to compose with creating my own self and reaching "authenticity" and "fulfillment." Furthermore, with our cultural shift from concern for our *soul* to worry about our *self,* we get confused thinking about guilt and sin.

We can get to feel that it's simpler to just move on when we fall. After all, Jesuit theologian Piet Schoonenberg pointed out, refusing to heed the summons to get up and move on humbly and hopefully is perhaps the deepest sin. But we first acknowledge our sin, for we need a horizon beyond just rising up humbly. That horizon is progress in our love for God and for our others—and even for our enemies.

But should we get depressed "confessing the same things, over and over," as one notably holy person lamented—we recognize the subtle temptation of perfectionitis. *No matter how good I am, I'm not good enough. Ever.* That's a devilish lie, of course. I am always my sinful self—and good enough for Christ to come redeem, and good enough for God the Father to love as His own child. So I rise today, humbly and hopefully, and turn to the next good thing to do.

The next good thing to do, I intend will be what God gives me to do. St. Paul told the Corinthians: *God has reconciled himself to us through Christ and has given us the ministry of reconciliation.*[121] It was true of Paul and of his Corinthians. And it is true of us: Others have handed on to us this disciplined asceticism of love of God and neighbor and self. Now it is our turn, and we do well to make sure we are energetic in pursuing it.

The best way of all was sketched by St. Paul for the Thessalonians: *Always be joyful. Pray constantly. And in all things, give thanks. This is God's will for you in Christ Jesus.*[122]

This is the everyday embrace of the disciplined asceticism of love and a profoundly positive purpose in life: *Make a tree good, and the fruit will be good.*[123] The fruits are the virtues, external enactments of grace within. Handling our usual faults and sins is the work of the daily Examen, and the place to start now is with the Gifts Examen, living the fruits of the Spirit.

Touchstones

- We have learned to live humbly and joyfully as sinners redeemed.
- The last step in repentance is accepting God's infinite love and mercy into our own selves and actions.
- We are tempted by our faults and failures to sloth, living dissed, and perfectionitis.
- We handle these by enacting the virtues—powers and authorities—God pours in us.

- We reject our culture's "authenticity" and "fulfillment" and open our hearts to God's ultimate gift to His sinful creatures: Himself.

- We have received this fire of love from others and now pass it on in our turn.

- All of this adds up to the disciplined asceticism of love of God and neighbor and self.

Always Beginning

PART THREE

Living Ignatian Spirituality

Introduction

It's true that in Paris Ignatius and his university companions began a friendship in the Lord that evolved into a big religious order. It's also true that they studied theology after completing their Master of Arts.[124] Their thinking grew to be learned, Aristotelean, and scholastic. They were known and honored as Masters of Paris.

They never thought of themselves that way, though. They came to think of themselves first of all as Companions of Jesus—all of them, together. They brought a genuinely new thing in the Church: *communitas ad dispersionem*, a community meant to be scattered to bring people to Christ.

Furthermore, the spirituality of these Masters of Paris, beginning with Ignatius', was grounded not in their learning, but in the direct, personal experience of God in Christ that they shared in making the *Spiritual Exercises*. Always in the Church, though: the early Jesuits believed what all the orthodox believed. Ignatius had had to prove that a dozen times before the Inquisition, and then the Companions had to get the pope's approval because of other Catholics' worries about their orthodoxy.

The upshot of all of this is that Ignatian spirituality is not first shaped by a seeker's context or level of learning. It is shaped by their direct experience of God in Christ as they pray and labor through the *Spiritual Exercises*.

We have been appreciating Ignatian spirituality as the experience of a disciplined asceticism of love of God and neighbor and self. This description would fit the spiritual traditions of monastery, friary, and cloister, too. But these spiritualities, distinct in their contexts and purposes, conform to their foundations. They create regular rhythms of prayer and common worship, specific kinds of work, study, and creativity, and unique times of silence, solitude, and community. Consequently, the disciplined asceticism of these religious calls for principles, norms, and practices appropriate to their context and designed for its specific purposes. These are as different from Ignatian spirituality as they can be.

For from the beginning, the spirituality defined by the principles, norms, and practices of *Exercises* required no specific places or purposes. On the contrary, from the beginning, this spirituality has shaped lives in universities, chanceries, missions in the new world, in very ordinary family life, and in hospitals and parishes.

In all of these settings, Ignatian principles, norms, and practices are designed to shape a person's *relationships*—first with God, then promptly with each friend and enemy God puts into a life. And today, because we think of self as unfinished and coming to be in a culture of deep individualism—today, we need principles, norms, and practices that give proper shape to a relationship with ourselves, as well—never apart from but constantly embedded in family and a web of friends, communities of faith, and the others in our lifeworld.

So our contexts differ vastly and we seekers living in them differ quite as much from one another. Yet we are all living a spirituality with identifiable characteristics. We experience these characteristics in our own head, heart, and hands. And we see others display them and listen to others explain their experiences in terms of this spirituality.

Describing that spirituality—that distinctive way of finding God in all things to praise, revere, and serve Him—is what I am doing here.

Of course, my own experience shows. But what I detail here are deep lessons learned in long, intimate living with scores of soberly creative Jesuit companions and in companioning many scores of men and women who have let me share their experiences in making *Exercises* and in spiritual direction during sixty years of practice. I do not mean to claim that any who practice this spirituality display all its characteristics fully and for all to see, though on close inspection, some come very close.

I do mean to claim that I am describing how many women and men live: the hopeful, persevering, day-by-day enactment of this special disciplined asceticism of love of God and neighbor and self that we call *Ignatian.*

24. The Experiences Characteristic of Ignatian Spirituality

1. First is an established personal relationship with God our Creator and Lord. Ignatius talks less about "seeking God" and more about "doing what pleases His divine Majesty," in the understanding that God is at each instant active in His creation. God has come seeking us—each and all of us.

- We live in what ignatian spirituality calls an "intimacy with God." This is not an idea or a feeling; it is a quality of our mature conscious life and the enactment of the Contemplation for Love: God giving gifts, remaining in them, acting in them, and sharing divine Being and all else—intelligence, freedom, creativity, personhood in relations.[125] We have appreciated that in prayer. And living aware of God in our life and of our life in God is our "mindfulness."
- We therefore seek a busy God, expecting to find God in all things. This is what we mean by "doing God's will." As Jesus put it: *By himself, the Son can do nothing; he can do only what he sees the Father doing."*[126] We want to walk like this, with the Father.
- The principle we live by is that every good thing we do praises, reverences, and serves God.
- We *walk humbly with the Lord,*[127] aware that we are and have nothing of ourselves—*It is all God's work.*[128] This means that we will not grow so attached to any idea or conviction, thing or person, that we let this creature stand between us and our God.
- We appreciate our own life and the lives of those around us as the gift of an infinitely loving God. All is freely given.
- God's will for us—what He is hoping in eternity we will be doing and will become—is a *personal* matter, not just part of a "plan" for the whole cosmos. We freely talk to God and say what we need to say.
- We try to keep aware that we belong to the earth. We want it kept beautiful and we anticipate *a new heaven and a new earth, the dwelling of God with humankind.*[129]

2. We develop by God's grace a personal relationship with Jesus Christ. We pray daily in the gospels, considering and contemplating the life of Jesus of Nazareth and His people.

- We beg insistently for the grace to "know Him more clearly, love Him more dearly, and follow Him more nearly."
- We beg this grace aware that God's response will not make us someone we are not, but will call on us to enact always more faithfully and generously our concrete gifts of head, heart, and hand.
- When our heart is genuinely on fire with His love, we pass it on by enacting His loving gifts. And we look for ways to bring others to Him.
- Each of us has a call in Christ and when we respond, we find ourselves building in our intimate lifeworld a kingdom of justice, peace, and love.
- We have chosen to accept Jesus' choosing us. *I have called you friends* means He and He alone is the mediator between our humanity and the divinity—and each of us feels Him *my Savior.*
- As we mature, the persistence of evil impresses us more and we come to realize that only Jesus Christ could defeat it. Our sound hope is in His rising in our flesh and destroying sin and death.
- We live glad that we were chosen in eternity to be His brothers and sisters, whom God *decided beforehand were to be the ones destined to be molded to the pattern of His Son.*[130]
- Being with Him means we accept membership and are loyal to His people, the Church—generously and magnanimously.
- The living summary of all of this is our yearning to *love one another the way He has loved us*—with all the threatening and glorious experiences such loving might bring us to.[131]

3. As our Master did, we pray daily in characteristic ways. We pray because the Lord Jesus told us to *ask* and to *seek,* and said that we are to *pray always.*[132]

- We ask the Lord for what we need and want, for the Church and our families, and for our nation, confident in our hope. We petition the Lord constantly, candidly and without fear or doubt. This marks our prayer discipline.
- We also live aware that Jesus taught His disciples: *When you pray, go to your private room, shut yourself in, and so pray to your Father who is in that secret place, and your Father who sees all that is done in secret will reward you.*[133] We understand this as mental prayer in union with God.
- We live aware of the faithful, steady action of the Holy Spirit, whom we know as a divine Person.
- Importantly in our ascetical life, we reflect every day on our thoughts, words, and deeds, applying the pattern of the Examen established in the *Spiritual Exercises.*
- We have learned to enter into Jesus of Nazareth's experiences by reflecting on the persons involved (Jesus first, of course), what is said, and what is done. At all appropriate times, we try to enter into ignatian contemplation this way, always wanting to share the human experience of the Redeemer.[134]
- Aware of God acting in all His gifts and discerning the next good thing to do, we become contemplatives in action.
- Most of the time, we pray the prayer of consideration, weaving Word and world together, as we did in the experience of *Spiritual Exercises.*
- Consequently, we easily follow an ignatian pattern of the *lectio divina:* read, *consider,* pray, and *discern.*

4. As we mature, we come to a quiet but deep sense of sin in world and self. We grow clearer and clearer how we breach the love that flows between God and ourselves by our imperfect response to that Love.

- The mature learn that excessive profit-taking has seriously harmed our economy and democracy; our culture's sexual license is not "freedom" but slavery; and that racial prejudice permeates our breathing in and out. We look to Jesus Christ for courage and The People of God for wisdom.

- Sin-in-the-world becomes sin-in-us the way polluted air fills each one's lungs or the way lead-poisoned water infects our bodies. This is how we understand *the law of sin that lives inside my body* that Christ is saving us from.[135]
- We live repentant lives, letting our sinning humble us but never make us desolate. We live contrite but not guilt-ridden, and remembering sin fills our hearts with God's loving forgiveness. Through the working of the Holy Spirit, our sinfulness moves us to be meek, gentle, and compassionate.
- We live aware that we have the freedom to turn away from God. We know that in some concrete case an attachment could lead us to choose some thing or person against God's will.
- We might excuse all other serious sinners, whomever, on the grounds of their DNA, rearing, and the harshness of their life world. But when we think of it, we know one person who is able deliberately to sin mortally: me.
- Through our ordinary days, the virtue of *fear of the Lord* fills us with reverence and awe at His almighty wisdom and power—and with trust in Jesus Christ's promise that He is *with us all days.*[136]

5. We can tell stories of our own experiences in living the principle and foundation. We have experienced challenges that forced us to choose consciously to remain faithful to God in Christ and to look forward to eternal life.

- We live day to day with a quiet heart, content with who we are and where the Lord has brought us, and trusting the guidance of the Holy Spirit.
- We have decided that, with God's grace, we will never prefer any created thing to the love of our Creator.

- We are aware of *making progress* in following the will of God for us and in showing our family, friends, and communities how much God loves us.
- We praise and thank God for everything in our life and experience—for the thousand wonders and miracles. Yet we let no creature block God's loving presence in us and in all things.
- We have grown aware that in God's will for me are certain experiences that I *must engage in,* even for long periods of time, or that I *must not engage in* at all.
- We are passionately attached to many things—our ideas and viewpoints about the faith or politics, our friends and relationships, our own place and time, and much else. Yet we are so free within these attachments that we are ready to let go of any of them that has become an obstacle in our love and service of God.

6. We have learned that mature disciples live aware of ongoing discernment. We have developed our own way of discerning, with the help of a good spiritual companion or guide.

- We discern steadily because it is a condition of making progress in our lives, both interiorly and as members of the Christian community.
- We mean to think with the Church and try to be responsible in keeping up with Church teaching.
- Though the text of *Spiritual Exercises* does not use the language of head, heart, and hands, the entire approach of *Spiritual Exercises* enacts this holistic way of making choices and reflecting on them.
- We sometimes feel that a definite spirit is leading us—loving, spiteful, fearing, yearning—and we are prepared to decide whether to follow it or not.
- We are perhaps helped in this by the "Rules for the Discernment of Spirits."[137]

7. We live visibly as Christians, disciples of Jesus Christ, active members of a Christian community.

- We keep about us signs that we belong to the Mystical Body – wearing a cross or medal that is more than an ornament, carrying a holy card or prayer in our wallet, displaying enriching art in our home and office.
- We want to love the Church and God's people as Jesus has shown us to – passionate and compassionate, challenging and forgiving, correcting with love. We do not let its need for reform diminish our loyalty to the Church.
- In our civil and political opinions, we try to honor the Church's social teaching, for instance, about immigration, war and peace, care for the poor, racism, and care for the earth.
- We are ready *to explain the reasons for our hope* when people ask, and try to do it *with courtesy and respect and with a clear conscience.*[138]
- We pray constantly with the whole church for the whole church and join the Ignatian practice of praying the Morning Offering.
- When occasion arises, we are ready to lead others to reflect and pray.

The enactment of all of this emerges in the stable mindset that we are called to do more, live expecting that we will find God acting in all things, and yearning to cooperate always better with our divine Creator and Redeemer. Day by day, we do this, humbly asking to know Jesus more clearly, love Him more dearly, and follow Him more nearly.

25. The Gifts Examen[139]

We are a people much given to reflecting on and examining ourselves. Too many of us are also much troubled by a negative self-image and by the vice of sloth. As a consequence—though there are other causes—we do not easily continue the Ignatian Examen with its focus on ridding ourselves of faults and failures.

Mature disciples are also determined to keep making progress, maturing and deepening in our disciplined asceticism of love of God and neighbor and self. We will not do that unless we reflect daily and with some order on our selves. We need a way and form to do that.

The Gifts Examen has provided it well for those who have tried it. Its usefulness is clear when we reflect that we grow by developing good habits. These have names: the virtues, powers, and authorities that are infused into us by the Spirit.

When the virtues are practiced—when we are patient, kind, courageous, wise—we have developed character. This character, St. Paul explained, belongs to those whom God *predestined to be conformed to the image of His Son.* He wrote that *those whom he predestined he also called; and those whom he called he also justified; and those whom he justified he also glorified.*[140] So St. Irenaeus can state that "the glory of God is the human fully alive."

Staying fully alive means being very active, and being active as an upright disciple of Christ means doing a lot of good things—virtuous things. So, when mature disciples examine themselves, rejecting negative self-image and the vice of sloth which disses our gifts and downplays them, we necessarily look at the virtues we are practicing.

And the powers. Our powers begin with believing, hoping and loving even those who do not love us in return. They reach into being empowered to counsel our young and our friends. Among many other powers that we have, courage to remain faithful in hard circumstances stands out.

As for authorities, each of us can recite the Creed as though we had written it: it is *our* Creed. We are authorized to announce the Good News to others, to let them know that we expect to live forever in joy with God and the saints. We need no license or certificate; our Baptism and Confirmation has established us as representatives of the Kingdom of God on earth—and of the kingdom to come.

So what we want to examine is how we are living that out. And the most sensible way to do that is to ask whether we are practicing the virtues that we are given—just those powers and authorities we need to do what we are called to do this day.

A good way to begin is with what St. Paul names "the fruits of life in the Spirit—alluding to Jesus' remark about making a tree good and its fruits will be good: *love, joy, peace, patience, goodness, kindness, trustfulness, gentleness, and self-control.*[141]

THE GIFTS EXAMEN

Each day, I set myself to live the gifts that the Holy Spirit gives to me.

On rising:
I thank God for the day, say the Creed to myself, and make the Morning Offering.[142] I recall the day's virtue.

During the day:
My job is my vocation; my work, God's work. I try to live my faith, hope, and divine love in family, work, and town. And I focus today on one virtue or gift.

In the evening:
I examine how I lived today's virtue, using St. Ignatius' five points. One: I thank God for all His gifts; Two: ask for honesty and insight; Three: check how I did; Four: ask God to forgive and heal; and 5: look forward to tomorrow.

The gifts of the Spirit, taking them one each day of the week: Sunday, love; Monday, joy; Tuesday, peace; Wednesday, patience; Thursday, kindness and goodness; Friday, trustfulness; Saturday, gentleness and self-control.

The infused gifts and virtues:
Before God, Theological virtues: faith, hope, and love.
Before your life-world, Cardinal virtues: prudence, justice, fortitude, and temperance.
Before all the people you love and are loved by, Gifts of the Holy Spirit: wisdom, understanding, counsel, fortitude, piety, knowledge, and fear of the Lord.

SUNDAY

I accept the Gift of Love

On rising:

I praise You, God of Love, for a day of rest. Your Holy Spirit has poured into my soul the gift of divine love. So gifted, I pray my morning prayers.

During the day:

- I will act in this spirit of love -- for my family N.N., my friends N.N., my co-workers N.N.
- I embrace the work You give me this day; I mean to do everything lovingly.

In the evening:

- I thank You for the love You gave me this day and remember Your gifts.
- Trusting Your forgiving love, I look at what I felt and thought, and what I said and did, asking if I acted in love?
- Heal me, Lord Jesus, and keep me close to You and never let me be parted from Your love.

Grant me, Lord, a restful night and a peaceful death.

MONDAY

I embrace the Gift of Joy

On rising:
I praise You with joy in my heart, Lord, because I know that my Redeemer lives. So gifted, I pray my morning prayers.

During the day:

- I will live joyful and be happy with my family, N.N., my friends N.N., my co-workers N.N.
- I embrace the work You give me this day; I mean to do everything cheerfully and enjoy it.

In the evening:

- I thank You for the joy I have known this day, recalling the special times of it.
- Begging the joy of insight, I look at what I felt and thought, and what I said and did—with joy?
- Heal me, Lord Jesus, and keep always in the joy of knowing that I am joined to You.

Grant me, Lord, a restful night and a peaceful death.

TUESDAY

I embrace the Gift of Peace

On rising:
I praise You, God of mercy, in the peace of this morning. You want no one to perish, but to forgive and save all. Hear my morning prayer.

During the day:

- I want to spread God's peace in my family N.N., among my friends N.N., and my co-workers N.N.
- I set myself to do whatever You give me today with peace in my heart and in all my actions.

In the evening:

- I thank you, Prince of Peace, for the times today when You shared Your own peace with me and us.
- Grant me to quietly acknowledge those times today when I refused to take Your peace into what I thought and felt, what I said, and what I did.
- Heal me, Lord Jesus, breathe on me Your gentleness and love; let me live in the peace of Your kingdom.

Grant me, Lord, a restful night and a peaceful death.

WEDNESDAY

I yearn for the Gift of Patience

In the morning:

- I praise You, God my Father, for Your patience with me and with all the wretched things that people do. Please hear my morning prayer.

During the day:

- I will deal patiently with every thing and with family N.N., friends N.N., and co-workers N.N.
- I embrace the work You give me to do today, asking that I may act as patiently as you, my God.

In the evening:

- I thank You, Lord, for always being patient with my sins and failures.
- Trusting Your patience with me, I look at all I felt and thought, said and did, and ask: Was I patient with every thing and with all people?
- Heal me, Lord Jesus, in Your infinite compassion, and remain patient with me as I come to You.

Grant me, Lord, a restful night and peaceful death.

THURSDAY

I accept the Gifts of Kindness and Goodness

In the morning:

- I praise you, mighty God, for You are good to all You create and kind towards me. In Your kindness, hear my morning prayer.

During the day:

- I set myself to be kind to all—to my family N.N., my friends N.N., and my co-workers N.N. & I embrace the work You give me to do today, asking that I may constantly be kind and do good.

In the evening:

- You are so good, mighty God, and Your kindness marked what You gave me today.
- Relying on Your kindness, I look at what I felt and thought, and what I said and I did, and ask: Did I act out my gifts of kindness and goodness?
- Heal me, Lord Jesus, with your kindness and wrap me close with Your goodness. Amen.

Grant me, Lord, a restful night and peaceful death.

FRIDAY

I give myself to the Gift of Trust

In the morning:

- I praise You, almighty and eternal God, for You have brought me through the darkness of another night. In the new light, hear my morning prayer.

During the day:

- I trust Your care for us all, for my family N.N, for all my friends N.N., and my co-workers N.N.
- I entrust to You with all my heart the work I do this day. Make all things work together unto good.

In the evening:

- I thank you, mighty God, for moments today when I trusted Your loving care for me and for my world.
- Trusting that you will not let my sins ruin me or harm those whom I love, I ask where I took charge in what I thought and felt, in what I said and did.
- Heal me, Lord Jesus, teach me not to grasp for control but to trust entirely in Your loving care.

Grant me, Lord, a restful night and peaceful death.

SATURDAY

I commit myself to the Gifts of Gentleness & Self-control

On rising:

- I praise You, meek and humble Lord, for the gift of gentle self-control and with it, spiritual freedom. So gifted, I say my morning prayers.

During the day:

- I will keep mastery of myself and be gentle towards my family N.N., my friends N.N., and all my co-workers N.N.
- I embrace the work You give me this day; help me to do it all with gentleness and self-control.

In the evening:

- I thank You for self-mastery today and recall all the gentle things You gave me to experience.
- Begging You to stay with me, I check whether self-control marked all the things that I said, and what I did, and how I acted.
- Heal me, Lord Jesus, and let me turn over everything to You and live gently on the earth.

Grant me, Lord, a restful night and a peaceful death.

Endnotes

1. *Spiritual Exercises*, Annotation 1. Tetlow. Translations of Master Ignatius' Spanish marked 'Tetlow,' are citations from Ignatius Loyola: *Spiritual Exercises*, New York, Crossroads, 1992.

2. Master Ignatius laid these out in Annotations 18, 19, and 20.

3. *Spiritual Exercises*, Annotation 18. Tetlow.

4. James Hanvey, SJ, "Ignatius of Loyola: Theology as a Way of Living," drawn on 05.29.2020 from the Jesuit website, thinkingfaith.org/articles/20100730_1.htm *Spiritual Exercises*, [230].

5. John W. O'Malley, SJ and Timothy W. O'Brien, SJ, *Studies in the Spirituality of Jesuits*, The Jesuit Conference, Washington, DC, vol 52, no 3, Autumn 2020.

6. Romans, 12:5. Verbatim citations from scripture are put in italic to distinguish them as the Word of God.

7. Pedro Arrupe, SJ, *Essential Writings*, ed. Kevin Burke, Orbis Books, Maryknoll, NY, 2004, 173.

8. Ignatius Loyola, letter to Francis Borgia, 1545. Joseph A. Munitiz SJ and Philip Endean SJ, *Saint Ignatius of Loyola: Personal Writings*, Penguin Books, London, 1996, 160-61.

9. Kenneth is a real person but Kenneth is not his name. These events are real, though details are airbrushed like a television report: you don't see the face but you see the event. In the stories and incidents still to come, I use a name when a real person is involved, though very commonly the experiences are matched by others' experiences. Over years, I worked with a number of "Kenneth's." I leave unnamed Illustrative or typical examples: "A man who said he was depressed turned out to be in the spiritual desolation due to an unacknowledged resentment."

10. John J. English, SJ, *Spiritual Freedom*, Chicago, Loyola Press, 1973. Revised and enlarged edition, 1995.

11. William Barry, SJ and William Connolly, SJ, *The Practice of Spiritual Direction*, New York, HarperOne, n.d. (1982?).

12. Quote from Cardinal Archbishop Jorge Mario Bergoglio in Francesca Ambrogetti and Sergio Rubin, *Pope Francis: Conversations with Jorge Bergoglio*, New York, G.P. Putnam's Sons 2013, 57.

13. This was discussed for a while as the "dynamic" of the Exercises. See Joseph Veale, SJ, "The Dynamic of the Spiritual Exercises," *The Way Supplement*, 1952, p.3-18; found now at theway.org.uk/back/s052Veale.pdf; and Howard Gray, SJ, "Dynamics of the Spiritual Exercises," lectures found now at president.georgetown.edu/initiatives/spiritual-exercises/

A longer and more theological exploration was done by James L. Conner, SJ, et al.: *The Dynamism of Desire: Bernard J.F. Lonergan, S.J., on the Spiritual Exercises of Saint Ignatius of Loyola*, Institute of Advanced Jesuit Studies, Boston, 2006.

14. *Spiritual Exercises*, [54]. Munitiz and Endean. "The Colloquy is made, properly speaking, as one friend speaks to another, or as a servant to his master; now asking some grace, now blaming oneself for some misdeed, now communicating one's affairs, and asking advice in them." Translations marked like the present one, 'Munitiz-Endean,' are citations from Joseph A. Munitiz SJ and Philip Endean SJ, *Saint Ignatius of Loyola: Personal Writings*, Penguin Books,

London, 1996. Those without translator, like the following endnote, are fresh translations or paraphrases by the author.

15. *Spiritual Exercises*, Annotation 15.

16. A computer search for discussion in our current culture of "familiarity with God" turns up scores of clearly negative entries from up and down the scale of sophistication, beginning with, "The Danger of Familiarity with God," and "Over-familiarity with God," and a warning that "Familiarity Breeds Contempt." Only the fifty-fourth entry asks "Is if OK to be familiar with God?" In this search and discussion, Ignatian and all Catholic spiritualities are directly and emphatically counter-cultural.

17. *Spiritual Exercises*, [234].

18. The basic insight into this "dialogue" was first proposed by Erich Przywara SJ. See *Deus Semper Maior: Principio y Fundamento*, Spanish translation, 2014 of the French original. [Rare book; no further biographical information.]

19. John 14:6.

20. 1 Corinthians 3:16.

21. Galatians 2:20.

22. The notes were translated into Latin and submitted for papal approval, which came on 31 July 1548. Five hundred copies were then printed. Master Ignatius stored them in his office and decided whom to give them to (not every Jesuit who asked received).

23. Note that the tradition of the Preached Weekend Retreat continues strong in the middle states and is coming back after falling off a bit in other areas. See Joseph A. Tetlow, SJ, "The Preached Weekend Retreat: A Relic or a Future?" in *Studies in the Spirituality of Jesuits*, vol. 48, no. 1, January, 2016. PDF Available online: ejournals.bc.edu/index.php/jesuit/article/view/9522

24. Since well before the 1980s, the Oblates of the Virgin Mary (OMV), have also given Ignatian retreats and spiritual direction. The congregation was important to the Church and especially to the Jesuits in the early 1800s, when the Society was restored after forty years of suppression. The Oblates had kept alive the tradition of one-to-one direction and helped the restored Jesuits pick it up again.

25. The story of changes from the retreat preached in the houses to the retreat made as Exercises in Daily Life is detailed in Joseph Tetlow, SJ, "The Remarkable Shifts of the Third Transition," *The Way Supplement*, 95 (1999), 18–30. Found now at theway.org.uk/back/s095Tetlow.pdf

26. This was not exactly new: The First Companions Peter Favre and Francis Xavier did exactly this in Parma, Italy, in 1541. Fabre reported to Ignatius that they gave simple Exercises to groups of ten or so and then encouraged them to pass it on, so that now, he said, we see our retreatants' "children and grandchildren," as they pass it on.

27. See the excellent story of the BRIDGES program on the web. The story it tells has been repeated in similar ministries over and over again all around the nation. "The Story: BRIDGES Foundation of St. Louis" found at bridgesfoundation.org/232-2/ Most Holy Trinity Ignatian Spirituality Center in San José is at Spiritualminstry@MHT-Church.org

28. Many announce the study of things ignatian—"discernment" is big just now—but cannot reasonably claim to be formation programs. And "ignatian" seems to have become something of a brand with very slippery content. It's hard to know what some programs involve. The Carmelite and Ignatian program at avila-institute.org requires making the 19th Annotation retreat and a course on discernment. And Steubenville University "seeks to meet the growing demand for trained spiritual directors" by yet another academic program, "Franciscan and Ignatian," whose founding director was trained in an Ignatian program. franciscan.edu/franciscan-university-launches-school-of-spiritual-direction/ Perhaps we have not been clear enough about what "ignatian" and "formation" actually mean and require.

29. *Spiritual Exercises*, [47], Tetlow.

30. Bernard Haring, CSsP, *Free and Faithful in Christ*, New York, Crossroad, 1978, 100.

31. Ignatius of Loyola, *Autobiography*, para. 30.. Munitiz and Endean, 26.

32. *Spiritual Exercises*, [234].

33. Ignatius does not use the term "supernatural" in his text. His use of the theological term "grace" commonly names a place where the seeker's action and God's action intersect: grace "to remember his sins" [25]; "grace to imitate Him" [139]; and most typically, "ask grace of God our Lord that all my intentions, actions and operations may be directed purely to the service and praise of His Divine Majesty" [46].

34. Paul VI, *Octogesima Adveniens*, 1971, paragraph 35.

35. *Gaudium et Spes, The Church in the Modern World*, paragraph 40.

36. Romans 13:1.

37. Romans 12:2.

38. Luke 12:57.

39. Barry and Connolly, *The Practice of Spiritual Direction*, 9.

40. See Barry and Connolly's lucid treatment in chapter 6: "Development of Relationship and Resistance."

41. See Robert Bellah, et al. *Habits of the Heart: Individualism and Commitment in American Life, University of Berkeley Press, Berkeley, CA, 1985.*

42. David Riesman with Nathan Glazer and Reuel Denney, Yale Univ. Press, New Haven CN, 1950.

43. Barry and Connolly, 114.

44. Barry and Connolly, 121.

45. Romans 12:1. When we are content ourselves with all God gives us, we hope to hear a seeker making progress in mature self-acceptance and satisfaction.

46. Matthew 25:35.

47. See *Evangelii Gaudium, The Joy of the Gospel*, paragraph 35, where Pope Francis describes

today's Gnosticism as "a purely subjective faith whose only interest is a certain experience or a set of ideas and bits of information which are meant to console and enlighten, but which ultimately keep one imprisoned in his or her own thoughts and feelings."

48. *St. John Paul II, The Redemption of the Body and Sacramentality of Marriage (Theology of the Body)*, Rome, Libreria Editrice Vaticana, 2005. This series of lectures was also published as *Man and Woman He Created Them: A Theology of the Body*, 2006, Boston, MA: Pauline Books & Media.

49. Matthew 7:17.

50. Richard J. Hauser, S.J. *In His Spirit: A Guide to Today's Spirituality*, Paulist Press, New York/ Mahwah, N.J., 1982. p. 5.

51. See Helen Orchard, "The Creature and the Sovereign Self: The Anthropology of the Spiritual Exercises and Contemporary Spiritual Narcissism," *The Way*, vol. 59, no. 1, January 2020, 11–21. Available on 08.21.2020 at thinkingfaith.org/articles/creature-and-sovereign-self

52. See the government report on "The 'Loneliness Epidemic,'" a summary of surprisingly extensive studies on the issue. Available on 10.2.2020 at Health Resources and Services Administration, hrsa.gov/enews/past-issues/2019/january-17/loneliness-epidemic

53. John Staudenmaier, SJ, exposed this "therapeutic individualism," by weaving together "three related things: (1) a sense of one's self as the primary or, more extremely, the only valid arbiter of belief and commitment; (2) a correlative mistrust of both the benefits and demands of one's received traditions or of interdependence with family, friends, or fellow citizens; and (3) a strong focus on acquiring self-knowledge and behavior modification in order to correct one's dysfunctional characteristics." From "To Fall in Love with the World: Individualism and Self-Transcendence in American Life," *Studies in the Spirituality of Jesuits*, 26/3, 1994, 2.

54. The authors add: "What we can or should be swings in endless response to the demands of the moment. Postmodern life provides one identity option after another, implicating a dizzying array of possibilities for the self." Jaber F. Gubrium and James A. Holstein, "The Self in a World of Going Concerns," *Symbolic Interaction*, Vol. 23, No. 2, pages 95-115, 95. Accessed on 04.22.2020 at sociology.missouri.edu/sites/default/files/people/self_in_a_world_of_going_concerns

55. Thomas Clarke, SJ, "Ignatian Prayer and Individualism," *The Way, 8*. Available on 07.20.2020 at theway.org.uk/Back/s082Clarke.pdf

56. Ignatius of Loyola to Francis Borgia, Duke of Gandia, 1545. Monitiz and Endean, *Ignatius Personal Writings,* 160. "I like to think that when persons go out of themselves and enter into their Creator and Lord, they enjoy continuous instruction, attention and consolation; they are aware of how the fullness of our eternal Good dwells in all created things, giving them being, and keeping them in existence with His infinite being and presence."

57. 1 Corinthians 3:16.

58. Luma Simms, "People and Their Relationships," *Public Discourse: The Journal of the Witherspoon Institute,* March 12, 2020. Drawn on 03.15.2020 from https://www.thepublicdiscourse.com/2020/03/60845/

59. Bernard Haring, *Free and Faithful in Christ*, p. 100. Emphasis added.

60. John 15:10 and 19.

61. Carlos is a real person and so is his quest for a job. Confidentiality is guarded by two things: first, names and details are changed and second, the spiritual experience described is quite common—which is what makes this illustration helpful.

62. Hanvey, SJ, "Theology as a Way of Living," drawn from thinkingfaith.org/articles/20100730_1.htm

63. *Spiritual Exercises* [230].

64. 1 Thessalonians 5:16.

65. In one linguistic analysis, communion is derived from the two Latin words *cum, with*, and *munire*. *Munire* means to strengthen, fortify, supply what is needed for a journey or a battle—all done *together, with one another*.

66. Galatians 5:1.

67. Matthew 11:29.

68. The story of these "Third Orders" is quite splendid but not well known. St. Catherine of Siena was a Third Order Dominican and so was Dante Alighieri. Michelangelo and Thomas More were Third Order Franciscans, as were Dorothy Day and Walker Percy. Actress Jane Wyman was buried in a Dominican habit. These Orders quietly continue to this day. Among those still functioning: Third Order of Saint Augustine, Oblates of Saint Benedict, Secular Order of Discalced Carmelites—then, Dominican, Franciscan, Mercy, Holy Trinity, Norbertines, Salesians, and Servites. There may be others.

69. Bernard Haring, *Free and Faithful in Christ*, New York, Crossroad, 1978, vol. 1, 100.

70. The word "spirituality" does not appear in the Council's major document on the Church, but its current reality is clear in many places. For instance: "The root reason for human dignity lies in man's call to communion with God." *Gaudium et Spes, The Church in the Modern World*, paragraph 19. Then the document declares that Christ lived, and the Church lives, "so that the world might be fashioned anew according to God's design and reach its fulfillment." Paragraph 2. Ignatian spirituality resonates with a great deal in the Council, declaring now that we are all created "men and women for others" whose purpose in life is to create a world of justice, peace, and love.

71. This is the significance of Annotations 2, 5, 15, 18, 19, and 20. The Kingdom contemplation will help anyone find "the attitudes we must acquire to reach perfection in whatever state of life God Our Lord may offer us for our choice." [135] Munitiz and Endean.

72. Master Ignatius describes Three Kinds of Humility [165] for a seeker making an election about state in life and manner of living. Specifically, he is describing the values embraced when a seeker chooses a manner of life like Francis of Assisi's. But humility of all three depths mark every life from the hermit's to the grandparents'.

We are considering here the Ignatian spirituality that marks the life of a seeker after making *Spiritual Exercises*. This seeker is looking to live an ongoing dialogue with God and to make always more progress. In this case, the humility of the seeker emerges in choices more like these: First kind [165] is humbly staying out of sin. Second kind [166] is being deeply indifferent and ready to accept whatever health, wealth, and happenings God gives. Third kind [167] is being *glad to share the sufferings that Christ has still to undergo for the sake of His body, the Church.* Not seeking suffering, even avoiding it when that is reasonable and possible, but accepting it with Christ when the Father asks us to accept it.

73. Galatians 5:1.

74. 1 Corinthians 3:16.

75. *Spiritual Exercises*, [54]. Tetlow.

76. See Leslie Woodcock Tentler, *American Catholics: A History*, New Haven & London, Yale University Press, 2010. The author describes American Catholics' experiences in both religious and civil life. The book notably enlarges readers' grasp of our religious experiences and the historical context of the development of American Catholic spirituality.

77. *Spiritual Exercises*, [18].

78. *Spiritual Exercises*, [238 to 260]. Here, Ignatius recommends praying about the virtues, [245 and 257]. The second method "is by contemplating the meaning of each word of a prayer." The third method is to say a prayer rhythmically. These are clearly the beginnings of mental prayer, as is the Gifts Examen, and open the way to make personal progress in prayer. Master Ignatius seems to have noted this, himself. [238].

79. Barry and Connolly, *The Practice of Spiritual Direction*, xiv.

80. Ignatius suggests this about the movements during the long retreat, [17]. Directors' experiences suggest the same is true for ongoing spiritual direction.

81. Matthew 5:48.

82. Pope Francis, *Laudato Si', On Care for Our Common Home*, 2015, para. 13. Now at vatican.va/content/francesco/en/encyclicals/documents/papa-francesco_20150524_enciclica-laudato-si.html

83. Paul VI, *Octogesima Adveniens, A Call to Action on the Eightieth Anniversary of Rerum Novarum*, 1971, 35. This social encyclical is third, after two earlier ones: Leo XIII's *Rerum Novarum, Rights and Duties of Capital and Labor*, in 1891; and Pius XI's *Quadragesimo anno, Forty years, On Reconstruction of the Social Order*, in 1931. Then *Paul VI's* was followed by the fourth: John Paul II's *Centesimus annus, The Hundredth year*, 1991. To this list should be added a fifth: Pope Francis' *Laudato Si', On the Care for Our Common Home*, 2015. This is the Church's "social teaching," which certainly forms a major part of the principles and norms that we must honor if we follow Master Ignatius in "Thinking with the Church" [352].

84. *Spiritual Exercises*, [5]. Tetlow.

85. *Spiritual Exercises*, Annotation 10. St John of the Cross, Ignatius' very late contemporary, created a classical application of these 'ways' to spiritual growth: purgative, illuminative, unitive. Ignatius did not think in these terms at all. He used them only here, explaining the discernment of spirits during *Exercises* of the First and Second Weeks. He never mentions the third stage,

the unitive way. Since he made the examen constantly to the end of his life, it may be that he understands that mature Christians live all our lives in the three ways interwoven, as the Holy Spirit leads us, obeying the Church's insistence on "ongoing conversion."

86. Master Ignatius never mentions the "unitive way." He certainly knew that those who accept the graces of *Spiritual Exercises* and who arrive at the "Contemplation for Love" able to benefit from it will be united to God not because they have earned it, but because God wants it. "Everything suggests that this same Lord of mine wishes to give Himself to me as far as He can according to His divine design." Tetlow, [230].

87. *Spiritual Exercises* [18].

88. *Spiritual Exercises* [189].

89. 1 Corinthians 3:16.

90. Romans 8:2.

91. "Friends in the Lord" is what the university students called themselves who created the Society of Jesus, the Jesuits. It is what *Compania de Gesù* actually means. See the article by Mark Lewis, SJ, in *America* at americamagazine.org/issue/553/article/friends-lord drawn on 02.03.2020.

92. The Colloquy ending the Contemplation on the Incarnation sets the pattern: "I will shape petitions out of what I have felt, leading to a closer following and imitation of our Lord now newly incarnate." [109]. This becomes so regular that by the Contemplation for Love, Ignatius can write simply, "I reflect about myself." [234]

93. See *Spiritual Exercises*, Ninth Rule of Discernment for the Second Week. [334]

94. Fourth and Fifth of the Rules of Discernment for the Second Week. [332 and 333]

95. Sixth of the Rules of Discernment for the First Week. [319]

96. These are well known Ignatian congregations, in the order of their founding: Sisters of Loreto (IBVM); 1609; Mary Ward's Congregation of Jesus (CJ); 1642; Sisters of St. Joseph (SSJ), 1650; Religious of the Sacred Heart of Jesus (RSCJ), 1800; Religious Sisters of Charity (RSC); 1815; the Oblates of the Virgin Mary (OMV), 1816; Faithful Companions of Jesus (FCJ), 1820; The Christian Life Communities (CLC) took its present shape, formally approved in 1971, but is the continuation of the Sodality of Our Lady that was established in 1563.

97. See the home page < Christian Life Community USA > clc-usa.org

98. 1 Thessalonians 5:11: *Therefore encourage one another and build up each other, as indeed you are doing.*

99. 1 Peter 3:16.

100. Matthew 5:24.

101. Donald L. Gelpi, SJ, has written extensively on conversion, its processes and consequences. See *The Conversion Experience*, Paulist Press, New York and Mahwah NJ, 1998; and *Committed Worship: A Sacramental Theology for Converting Christians*, 2 vols., Collegeville, MN: Liturgical Press, 1993. See also Walter Conn, *Christian Conversion: A Developmental Interpretation of Autonomy and Surrender*, New York, Paulist Press, 1986.

102. Romans 8:28.

103. *Spiritual Exercises*, [322].

104. Master Ignatius defines a "colloquy" as a conversation between friends or between a servant and master. Among other things, it includes "telling the other about one's concerns and asking for advice about them." *Spiritual Exercises*, [54]. Munitiz and Endean.

105. 1 Corinthians 12:9.

106. *Catechism of the Catholic Church*, 1266. "The Most Holy Trinity gives to the baptized ... the power to live and act under the prompting of the Holy Spirit through the gifts of the Holy Spirit."

107. *Gaudete et Exultate*, paragraph 21.

108. "Direction can be defined as the help that one man gives to another to enable him to become himself in his faith." Jean Laplace SJ, *Preparing for Spiritual Direction*, Tr. by John C. Guinness, Harrisonburg, VA, Franciscan Herald Press, 1988, 26. This early book was written to help instruct clergy as spiritual directors.

109. 1 Corinthians 12:7.

110. We *react* when we spontaneously react to something a seeker tells us, like exclaiming, "That was awful." Physically, we react when we flinch to a pin prick or jump to a loud noise behind us. We are reacting when we speak out before we have let ourselves consider for a moment. *Reacting* can also be resisting what they said, or even denying it—"But that's impossible!"—or jumping in to correct it. We *respond* when we have let what was said resonate in our mind and heart for a bit and then consider what to say and how. What we do say then, we judge what the seeker needs to hear—not what we feel we need to say. We are more likely to react when we are just beginning to give direction. As we get along, we discover that responding defends our peace of mind and heart, and the seeker, too.

111. Parker J. Palmer, *To Know as We Are Known: Education as a Spiritual Journey*, New York, HarperCollins, 1993, p. 14.

112. Ignatius of Loyola to Francis Borgia, Duke of Gandia, 1545. Monitiz and Endean, *Ignatius Loyola: Personal Writings*, 160.

113. *Spiritual Exercises*, [230].

114. Mary Ward is considered the founder of the congregations of women: IBVM, Loreto of Ireland, and the Companions of Jesus. Her reach was to the peripheries, so that women could serve the poor as men did in the Society of Jesus. Her work, like Ignatius', was suppressed, in 1631, and Mary Ward suffered vastly more at the hands of Cardinals and popes than did Ignatius. Happily, two Jesuit contemporaries, theologians Francisco Suárez and Leonard Lessius, were asked around 1615 for their opinion on the new way of proceeding by women and both praised it highly—though of course it had to be approved by a bishop (Lessius) or perhaps by the pope (Suarez), as the Jesuits' had been. The way of life ultimately got papal approval in 1703.

115. 2 Corinthians 5:14.

116. Philippians 2:13.

117. A visit to the *Greater Good Science Center* at the University of California at Berkeley is very instructive. Now at greater@berkeley.edu

118. I developed this in *Always Discerning*, Chicago, Loyola Press, 2016. See Part Ten: Discernment and Desolation, 195 – 214.

119. *Spiritual Exercises*, [234]. Munitiz and Endean.

120. 2 Corinthians 4:7

121. 2 Corinthians 5:15. We also learned this: "We must know Christ as the source of grace in order to know Adam as the source of sin." *Catechism of the Catholic Church*, para. 388.

122. 1 Thessalonians 5:16.

123. Matthew 7:17 and 12:33.

124. Ignatius, himself, studied for ten years, the last year and a half on theology. He began in Barcelona (1524-25) studying the *trivium*: grammar, logic, and rhetoric, necessarily opening the question of how we know the truth. He moved to the universities in Alcala and Salamanca (1526-27) to study the *quadrivium*, which included arithmetic (number), geometry (number in space), music (number in time), and astronomy (number in space and time). These gave students the basis for right thinking, which prepared them to study physics, metaphysics, and moral philosophy, the subjects of the master's degree. In Paris, he received the BA (1533) and the Master's Degree (1535). The Companions could study theology in Paris, one of the four places then licensed by the Holy See (Cambridge, Oxford, and Rome were the others).

125. *Spiritual Exercises*, [230].

126. John 5:19.

127. Micah 6:8. *And what does the Lord require of you but to do justice, and to love kindness, and to walk humbly with your God?*

128. 2 Corinthians 5:18.

129. Revelations 21:3.

130. Romans 8:29.

131. John 13:34.

132. Matthew 7:7; Luke 18:1.

133. Matthew 6:6.

134. More recently mature Ignatian prayer moves instinctively to apply the Grammar of Experience. This development seems to be inchoate and piecemeal, but the fruits of this way of considering the human experience of Jesus of Nazareth are showing up more and more in books on Ignatian spirituality.

135. Romans 7: 23: *I see that acting on my body there is a different law which battles against the law in my mind. So I am brought to be a prisoner of that law of sin which lives inside my body.* Translation in *The New Jerusalem Bible*.

136. Matthew 28:18.

137. *Spiritual Exercises* [313, 328].

138. 1 Peter 3:15.

139. This is the text of a pamphlet by Joseph A. Tetlow, SJ, printed at Our Lady of the Oaks Jesuit Retreat House in 2018. It is an instance of the change suggested by Master Ignatius in Spiritual Exercises to examining virtues rather than vices. [245]

140. Romans, 8: 30.

141. Galatians, 5: 22.

142. The "Morning Offering" is the prayer of a movement—the Apostleship of Prayer—begun by the spiritual guide of young Jesuit seminarians in 1844. This worldwide effort has continued for 175 years. Here is the classical form of the prayer: "O Jesus, through the Immaculate Heart of Mary, I offer You all my prayers, works, joys and sufferings of this day for the intentions of Your Sacred Heart, in union with the Holy Sacrifice of the Mass throughout the world, in reparation for sins, for the intentions of all [our associates] my relatives and friends, and in particular for the intentions of our holy father, the pope. Amen." The pope's monthly intention is readily found on the web.